How to Raise Viking Children
and Other Tales of Woe

HOW TO RAISE
VIKING
CHILDREN
AND OTHER TALES OF WOE

by Troy Maynard
of VeryVocalViking.com

Foreword by Dr. Alex Service, Ph.D.

Very Vocal Press, Bloomington IN 2017

ISBN-13: 978-0-9995159-0-7

Editing by Lynae Sowinski

Cover art by Justin Langford
senorrandom.tumblr.com

Published by Very Vocal Press
PO Box 903 Bloomington, IN 47402

Some selections in this book have previously
appeared in Limestone Post Magazine. You can
see these and other great articles at
limestonepostmagazine.com

Special thanks to
FIGID Press ~ figidpress.com

I dedicate this work to my amazing, wild, brilliant, colorful, and incredibly supportive family. You are the reason I am who I am and do what I do.

A special thank you to my Wonderful Wife, who so graciously puts up with me. You miraculously make it all possible, every day, and still manage to make it look so easy. You are amazing.

And big, burly Viking hug to all those friends who encouraged and pestered me for years to put this silliness into book form. Thank you. Really.

Table of Contents

Foreword

To say that I was honored at being asked to write a foreword for this work is an understatement. While I was reading *How to Raise Viking Children*, my reaction was a combination of heart-felt tears (only some of them tears of laughter) and the thought, "My husband has got to read this!"

My qualifications for writing this foreword are two-fold. First, like Wonderful Wife (whom you will meet in the pages of this book), I also am married to a big, tall, long-haired, impressive-bearded guy who is frequently called a Viking. (Although, in our grad school days, that really ticked him off. He was studying the Anglo-Saxon era of early medieval Britain, and he wanted to be called an Anglo-Saxon rather than a Viking. But for a variety of reasons, Anglo-Saxons haven't gotten the good historical press coverage that Vikings have. Few people name their sports teams "The Anglo-Saxons" or publish comic strips about Anglo-Saxons characters.) My second qualification is that I have a Ph.D. in medieval studies and my dissertation was titled *Popular Vikings: Constructions of Viking Identity in Twentieth-Century Britain.*

We're not in Britain, and time has rolled us inexorably into the 21st century. But many conclusions I reached in that dissertation are relevant to this Viking parenting manual. Chief of those conclusions is the fact that Vikings are people of extremes. The Vikings of our popular imagination are always *the most* at whatever they do.

Not that what they're doing is always a positive thing. As with witches, there are good Vikings and bad Vikings. But good or bad, Vikings are creatures of superlatives. If they are Vikings of the rape-and-pillage style, then they are the most ferocious and feared of all experts in rapine, pillage and slaughter. But Vikings can also be the most fearless and skillful explorers, the most talented, innovative ship-builders and navigators, the canniest and most successful merchants, the most eloquent (and the most self-praising) poets, and, of course, the bravest, most skilled of warriors.

In popular culture, Vikings' extreme nature is often shown in their dress sense. It manifests itself in helmets with over-sized horns or wings, and the tendency to run around dressed only in little furry shorts in sub-zero temperatures. In real life, Vikings past and present spend a lot less time wearing ridiculous helmets and furry shorts. But today and in the medieval world, a Viking man is unafraid to let his hair down (figuratively and literally). He will braid his beard when the situation requires it, he will bravely wear his heart upon his sleeve — and the medieval Viking men also frequently wore eye make-up, as we know from the 10th-century travel-writings of Ibrahim

Al-Tartushi. Viking masculinity is more wide-ranging and inclusive than popular images might lead us to believe.

The wit and wisdom found in this volume reminds me of passages in the *Hávámal* (*Sayings of the High One*), an Old Norse advice manual. The *Hávámal* tells us,

> *If a man takes with him a mind full of sense*
> *he can carry nothing better;*
> *riches like this on a stranger's road*
> *will do more good than gold.*

The *Hávámal* also advises,

> *Silent and thoughtful a king's son should be*
> *and bold in battle;*
> *merry and glad every man should be*
> *until the day he dies.*

How to Raise Viking Children is a work of true Viking spirit. It is true both to the popular Vikings of extremes, and to the Vikings who value sense, thoughtfulness and gladness. This is a Viking book not simply because its author is a big, beardy, Viking-looking guy. Just as Viking explorers fearlessly adventured on far seas, this book explores the adventures of parenting with unabashed love, with emotions deeply felt and deeply expressed, and with many a big, booming laugh. It is a fitting book for a Viking to have written.

Dr. Alex Service

Ph.D. in Vikingology

(or something like that)

Preface

I am blessed with an amazing family. My days are full with the love of an amazing woman and our three brilliant, hilarious children. As I realized our day-to-day discoveries and laughs were all too fleeting, eight years ago I decided to start capturing all our funny little interactions on Facebook. I wanted to share them so everyone could enjoy them, but mostly to save all those tiny snapshots of my incredible life so I could go back and enjoy them forever, even long after the kids had grown up.

At some point I also started writing out my own thoughts about how bizarre it is to be a parent. It shocks me every day how wonderful and difficult it is to be part of the "sandwich generation," seeing my kids grow up and become people, even as I watch my parents' health begin to fade. I see the Circle of Life play out in front of me every day. It's a powerful place to be and has opened my eyes to a lot of aspects of adulthood that are, at once, beautiful and terrifying.

Such is life.

Surprisingly, people seemed to really enjoy my thoughts and, especially, all the little funny snippets of our crazy family life. So much so that I started a blog to make them more easily accessible and readable.

But what could I name such a blog?

As I've grown out my hair and let my beard get longer and longer in recent years, people started to jokingly refer to me as a Viking. I've always loved Vikings and Norse mythology, so I embraced it wholeheartedly. And so was born The Very Vocal Viking.

For me it's not just a nickname. I absolutely respect those real-life people who identify as Vikings. I very much embrace and share many of their core philosophies. While much of the recent popular commercialization of Vikings is cartoon-like, with horned helmets and senseless violence, the truth of Vikings is much more simple, genuine, and sincere.

Most important to me is that being a Viking is a culture, a mindset, and a decision. It's not a nationality or race or anything to do with DNA or genealogy (sorry, racists). Being a Viking is a daily commitment to actively pursue strength (physical and mental), brotherhood based on actions not words, and the freedom to live an effective and intentional life. It's a deliberate and purposeful way of living. In that sense, I am a Viking.

With that said, please remember that above all, Art imitates Life.

These snippets of conversations and scenes from my life contained in this book are interpretations not meant to be taken literally. I've masked the names of my family members and everyone involved, partially for privacy but mostly because these characters have become bigger than life over the years. While many of the quotes in here are word-for-word, the truth is that most have been modified to be clearer, or to be more obvious, or to be less profane, or even just to be funnier. I've worked hard to keep them all in the same spirit in which they occurred, but some passages are more fictitious than others. I'll let you decide which is which.

I recommend reading this with an open mind and an open heart. Please enjoy these glimpses into the madness that is my delightful, charmed life.

Troy Maynard
VeryVocalViking.com

In Case of Fireball

In college, I lived in a dump. Actually, calling it a dump is an insult to dumps. It was a giant turn-of-the-century two-story duplex that sat squarely in one of those questionable old neighborhoods in town with that magical mix of poor college kids and poor families. The street parking was always crowded with junky cars. The air was often full of hearty laughter, or loud arguing, and occasionally with gunfire. It was always an adventure.

The house I lived in was literally falling apart. It didn't help that college boys lived there. I mean, sure, we crammed fourteen couches into a three-bedroom house. Sure we spilled a lot of beer. And, sure, we didn't clean often, or very well.

OK, I'm lying — we didn't clean at all. But sometimes one of us would date a woman who took pity on us. It seemed like a couple times a year one of these honorable souls would come in with buckets and sponges and brushes and soaps and sprays and rubber gloves, looking armed for war. And, bless their hearts, they'd pitch right in and clean up a bit. Or at least try. It was more like peeling back the first few layers. None of them stuck around to clean a second time. They all seemed to find a reason to break up soon afterward.

But you can't blame it on just us guys. The house itself had been horribly neglected for decades and was in shambles. To call it a "fixer-upper" was too gentle a term. The carpet was that tired '60s crushed shag that seemed to beg for mercy with each step. The linoleum was riddled with holes and peeled up at all of the edges. The staircases were narrow and steep. All the once-beautiful, old hardwood trim was scratched and etched and somehow permanently sticky. There were holes in the walls, the ceilings, the floors. I kid you not —

you could see the first-floor kitchen while sitting on the second-floor toilet. It was handy for having a conversation with the guy doing dishes, but not exactly a selling point.

Even with all those problems, the basement was worse. It genuinely looked like the set of a horror movie, and a low-budget one at that. The dingy, damp rooms had ridiculously low ceilings and rough walls like it had all been dug out by hand. The ancient furnace was a deep, sooty black — and noisy, and enormous. It commandeered almost half of the basement, with its squid-like tentacles stretching up and into the darkness of the sub-floor.

Our landlord was a friend of ours. Let's call him ... uh ... Bob. He was a little older than us and I barely knew him. He had rented the house himself when he was in school a few years prior. When Bob graduated, he bought the house because he saw a lot of potential. I'm not sure where he was hiding all that potential. All I could see were broken windows, splinter-happy floorboards, and several tetanus shots in my future. But who am I to argue with a budding Real Estate Tycoon?

All this to say that Bob cut us a deep discount on the price of rent with the condition that we would get up early every few Saturday mornings to help him fix up the place. I barely knew which end of a hammer to hold, but Bob said he had the home construction know-how. To be fair, some free on-the-job training was appealing and I could definitely use the break on rent. So, with our muscle and Bob's alleged expertise, we made elaborate renovation plans that would give *This Old House* a run for its money. Or not.

And, guess what — Bob really did know what he was doing. He might not have been a master carpenter or plumber, but he knew enough to make it all work. It was amazing to watch him plan a project, to make a list of supplies we needed, to go shopping and buy the stuff, and then do all the work to actually make it happen. For the first time in my life I was part of creating something of value and improving my world. It was a powerful and empowering education to see it all go from concept to completion, and to suddenly realize that even I could do that.

I learned so much from Bob over those few years about basic carpentry, flooring, finishing drywall, plumbing, installing carpet, etc. It was a fantastic education on basic home renovation. We made a good number of solid improvements to the house, including completely gutting that peek-a-boo bathroom down to the bare studs and starting over. It ended up being a pretty nice bathroom.

And, even more surprising to me, I made a pretty solid friend. Bob wasn't just our landlord but a really great guy. We had more fun doing the work on the house than I could have imagined, and he usually stuck around for an evening of hanging out with board games and some drinks. All in all my biggest lesson in all of this is — if someone is willing to teach you how to do something, you should take them up on it. It can truly change your life.

Of course, not all of the projects went so smoothly.

One bright and early Saturday morning, Bob woke us up, bleary-eyed and hungover, at the crack of 10 am. Looking back, we probably shouldn't have drunk so much the night before. But, hey, it was college. So, my good friend/roommate Bill and yours truly tried our best not to complain as we pulled on work clothes. Our third roommate, Buck, had conveniently slept over somewhere else. He was pretty good about not being around on renovation days. If I had been smarter, I probably would have tried to learn his trick.

Regardless, that particular day Bill and I dragged ourselves out of our warm, comfortable beds and followed Bob to the kitchen. Our job, he said, was to help him rip out the old, defunct 220-volt electrical line. Yes, "220" as in two-hundred-and-twenty volts of electrical power — enough to stop your heart and weld metal together. You know, no big deal.

Bob informed us that he had already disconnected the power in the basement, so our first step was to help him find where the 220 line came up through the floor. We poked around and eventually found it in the last place we thought it would be … behind the gas stove. You know, fresh, clean natural gas — as in explosive, flammable gas pulsing through metal pipes into our home. Right next to the 200-volt electrical line. No big deal.

I was shocked (see what I did there?). It seemed very odd to me to put the two so close to each other, almost literally touching. Very odd. And dangerous, as if the house had been designed by a madman.

(I have since been informed that this is a very common practice as stoves can be gas or electric and you might want either source there. But at the time, in my ignorance, it seemed insane. Frankly, it still does.)

But our intrepid group of weekend warriors would not be deterred. We pulled the stove away from the wall to give us plenty of room to work. The gas line was a rigid pipe for the first foot or so out of the floor, but, above that, it became a flexible coil hose that allowed for the stove to be pulled away. See, we knew what we were doing! It was designed to do this!

The 220 outlet was this ancient, dark-brown Bakelite monstrosity with three concentric slots for prongs that formed a tiny triangle pattern, kind of like a tiny warning sign. It was all very old school and oddly beautiful in its stark and angular design. Nevertheless, a quick pry with Bob's giant flathead screwdriver, and the casing was removed.

What the casing revealed was truly gorgeous. Six giant, glittering orange copper coils, two for each of the prong slots, sat twinkling before our eyes. I remember vividly how smooth and fresh the copper looked, so bright and shiny and tightly wrapped in such even little loops, all circling the center of the outlet. For as old as the thing was, I expected to find, at least, dirt and grime and maybe Jimmy Hoffa. The fact that not even dust was dumb enough to mess with this outlet was probably our final warning that we were out of our league.

Did we see the obvious danger? Sure. But we were big, manly men who knew how to control electricity. Were we going to admit we were afraid of 220 volts? Hell, no! Sure, it could stop our hearts or burn the skin clean off of our hands. Ha! We laughed in the face of such cowardice.

So, then, how to remove the outlet that's still clinging tightly to the wall? We looked and looked and found no tabs or knobs or clamps. How in the world was this thing still attached?

"Oh!" said my friend Bill, "I see it! There's a tiny screw in the center."

And there it was. A beautiful, tiny, silvery metal screw, deep in the center of all those gorgeous, shiny coils. Deep, deep in that little hollow between all those bright-orange, highly conductive copper coils. So easy. We had found it. No problem. Nothing left but to remove that tiny, harmless little screw.

For the record, I swear on all that's holy that I stopped right then to ask Bob if he was absolutely, positively sure he had disconnected the electricity. Like, *for sure*-for sure he disconnected it. To this day, I would be happy to swear on a Bible, take a lie detector test, to sign a solemn affidavit, whatever. I said it. I tried. With God as my witness, I tried.

Bob seemed puzzled by my lack of faith. I thought I saw a hint of indecision, a shadow of doubt, a minuscule question cross his face momentarily. But he shook his head confidently and assured me that he was not the kind of guy that would be messing with a 220 line if he was not completely certain he had disconnected it. And, he had always been right about stuff. Who was I to question my mentor?

Sigh.

In my mind, the next few seconds play back like a movie in slow motion. Bob was crouched next to the stove, slowly reaching his giant flathead screwdriver around the flexible gas line toward the tiny metal screw deep in those beautiful orange coils. Bill and I were standing obediently behind and to each side of him, intently studying the technique for future reference. Slowly, the screwdriver inched closer and closer. Bob exhaled somberly. The birds singing and insects buzzing outside suddenly fell eerily still. The house was almost frozen in time, blanketed in silence. I heard the clock ticking slowly, slowly.

And that's when all Hell broke loose.

There was the tiniest flash of bright white light and a really loud bang. Bob, who had been crouching, suddenly flew backward across the room between us and slid into the opposite cabinets 20 feet away. Bill and I instinctively turned and ran to him, checking to make sure he was OK. He was stunned but breathing. Bill checked Bob's pulse and found his heart was racing. We were relieved that he was alive but were concerned that he was still not responding to our excited questions. Do you know where you are? What day is it? What is your name?

Right about then, Bob came to his senses. I'd like to say he said something terribly witty or profound about his incredibly athletic leap backward across the kitchen, but in reality he just stared. His eyes got huge and his jaw hung wide open. Between you and me, it was a very odd expression and I was worried he'd gotten brain damage. It took a few moments for Bill and me to realize Bob wasn't actually looking at us, but staring in horror and amazement at something behind us.

I remember very distinctly that even before I turned around, I suddenly became aware of a very loud and constant "whooshing" sound behind me. And I recall noticing before turning that, for some odd reason, there was this beautiful orange light flickering all about the wall above Bob's head. I even thought maybe I detected the faint impression of heat radiating on my back. The entire moment was actually quite picturesque and beautiful and soothing in a way.

Then I turned around, and it was no longer soothing. Not soothing at all.

In that magical moment, my young and tender eyes were treated to a rare and life-changing view of a giant fireball, right there in our humble kitchen. The majestic cone of rippling flame purred contentedly as it projected onto the wall above the stove like a giant orange spotlight. All things considered, a very cool thing to see. So many people don't get to see an eight-foot cone of bright-orange fire, and certainly not in the safety of their home.

If you looked closely, you could see the sooty, black scorch marks on the flexible gas hose where the screwdriver had temporarily welded itself. The bright flash I saw had been the blue-white arc of electricity, jumping happily from the beautiful orange copper coils, to the steel screwdriver, and then to the flexible steel hose. The steel of the flexible hose was thin enough that the arc had also punched two tiny pinholes. Do you know what tiny pinholes in a flexible gas hose are good for? Well, they are just perfect to release two healthy, happy streams of natural gas, of course. And weren't we lucky that the bright white arc of electricity not only punched those delightful little pinholes, but was also nice enough to ignite it all and play a constant torch onto the wall?

And that, my friends, is how you make a fireball.

Let's take a moment, shall we? It's an ugly truth that there are times in everyone's life when you are tested. Whether the circumstances are your fault or not, at some point we are all thrust into pulse-pounding life-or-death situations. And, as much as we plan or prepare or theorize ahead of time, no one can truly predict how they will react. It is a well-established fact that Life will eventually throw something big and nasty at you someday. The Universe will test your mettle, and you just have to hang on for dear life.

This was one of those situations. My mettle was definitely tested. It was touch and go. Life and Death. Seconds matter. I had to react. So, friends, how did our brave hero rise to the occasion? How did my finely tuned instincts kick in and save the day? Well, actually ...

I ran.

I ran fast and hard and for as long as my chubby little legs would take me.

I'm not proud of my reaction, but I'm not ashamed either. It's a fully rational and reasonable reaction to run away from giant fireballs. It may not win me any awards for bravery, but in the end I still contend that running away is always a solid choice.

As I spun on my heel to make my inglorious getaway, it turns out the most complicated part of my escape was the fact that Bill was between me and the back door. I have in my head this perfect picture of him standing there behind me, frozen in shock, jaw agape and eyes wide, pointing halfheartedly at the fireball. But I was not frozen. In fact, I was moving with great haste. And he was very much in my path to safety.

Being the very large individual that I am, I learned long ago that acceleration is difficult and it should be respected once it is achieved. On the other hand, once I get some momentum, turning or changing direction is extremely difficult. And by extremely difficult, I mean to say it doesn't happen. I don't turn. Not in my vocabulary. I can slow down, sorta, or gradually stop, maybe — but turning is not on the menu.

In this particular situation, I was desperate to get to safety as quickly as possible. Bill says he doesn't remember the details, but my recollection is that I grabbed him by the shoulders, picked him up gently and then softly deposited him several feet to my right, out of my path. I then proceeded to exit the domicile at top speed.

I ran like my ass was on fire, and in this case, that was a serious consideration. I burst out the back door and across the back porch and jumped down the steps into the backyard and ran all the way to the alley. Once in the alley, completely off our property, I finally stopped and tried to catch my breath, hands on my knees, heart pounding in my ears like a jackhammer. I had made it. I had survived. I won this one. I would live to tell the tale!

And then, suddenly, the alley was a very quiet and lonely place to be standing by myself.

At that moment, for the second time in a very short span of time, I experienced an incredibly unique and rare occurrence. I had just outrun a giant fireball and imminent death, but now I had to ask myself several difficult questions. These were not your typical questions, not the kind of soul searching that you really ever want to experience. These were uncomfortable questions like, how far away should you be when your house explodes? Is the alley really far enough? Is it really worth running farther when you're kind of overweight and still out of breath? Was there time to call the police? Should I try to hide behind something like they do in the movies? Are you obligated to warn your neighbors your house is about to explode?

And with that last thought, my heart sank. It had finally occurred to me that my younger brother happened to live in the other half of our duplex. So not only were my friends in danger, but my flesh and blood, my one and only sibling, sat mere feet away from certain death, completely oblivious to his impending fiery doom.

Well, I thought to myself, it was nice knowing him.

What? What good would it have done for me to die, too?

It was logical. Wouldn't it be better for one of us to survive? I was just trying to carry on the family name. I had my lineage to protect here. I'm sure he would have totally understood.

Then it hit me. After he died, I was going to have to tell my mother that I didn't go back for him.

Sigh.

Now, I'm very large Viking. I don't fear many things. I can stare down a wild animal, or hold my own in a fight, and even change a diaper. But I'm not ashamed to admit I shook with fear at the thought of facing my mom. How would I possibly tell her that I could have gone back to save her only other son, but I had chosen instead to stay safely in the alley. How could I explain that it made so much sense at the time?

Sigh.

As I stood there, in the alley, cringing and waiting for the entire house to explode in a fiery rain of scorched brick and flaming bits of wood, it was suddenly very clear that I'd rather die than have to see the look on my mom's face when I told her.

So, back into the house I went, this time into the back door of the other half of the duplex.

When I say my brother lived next door, I mean to say that he and a dozen of his closest friends du jour all used it as a flop house. It was never really clear to me who actually lived there. It seemed to change day to day. I never knew who was on the lease or who paid rent. But there was always a small crowd of people and something going on. I wouldn't have wanted to live there myself, but it was a great social spot to have nearby.

Their sleeping arrangements were even more puzzling. All I knew was that everyone slept on mattresses and floors and wherever else they wanted in the various bedrooms upstairs. Who was sleeping with whom and where and why were none of my business and frankly I didn't want to know. All I knew that day, as I stood in the dining room of their half of the duplex, was that I had to get them all out of the building as quickly and efficiently as possible.

I quickly formulated a plan. I stood at the foot of the stairs up to the second-floor bedrooms and yelled with my big-boy voice, "GET OUT! WE BROKE A GAS LINE AND THE HOUSE IS ABOUT TO BLOW UP!"

To this day I question if that was the best phrasing I could have chosen. I was trying to be fairly direct, and I wanted to make it sound urgent. However, I only heard the faintest scratches of movement behind all the bedroom doors. So I tried again.

"EVERYONE GET OUT OF THE HOUSE RIGHT NOW! THIS IS NOT A JOKE! WE BROKE A GAS LINE AND THE HOUSE IS ABOUT TO EXPLODE!"

This time I distinctly heard several muffled voices behind doors asking, "Did he just say gas line?"

"YES, I SAID WE BROKE A GAS LINE! I AM TOTALLY SERIOUS! YOU ARE ALL GOING TO DIE!"

In hindsight, I'd ask for forgiveness for my dramatic slant on the last line — except that it got results. Madcap, fantastic results. I heard the gratifying sound of all three bedroom doors slamming open and what could have been up to maybe 20 people scattering in every direction. Several went out various windows onto the first-floor roof and then jumped to the ground. Most headed down the stairs toward my current location, so I decided I had done my civic duty for the day and made my retreat.

Once I was safely back in my favorite alley, I started to again ask myself those now-familiar questions. How far away should you be when your house explodes? Is the alley really far enough?

My questions quickly became moot when Bill calmly walked out of our back door and announced that the issue had been dealt with and we were all safe. A small relieved cheer went up from the crowd and we all filed back inside.

It turns out that Bob and Bill had made better use of their time than I had. Bob had immediately run up two flights of stairs to the attic to turn off the gas. No, it wasn't actually located in the attic. In the entire history of house design, since cavemen rubbed sticks together and built huts, no one has ever put the gas shut-off in an attic. But Bob's brain was on high alert and told him to check the attic, so up he went. Again, you don't get to choose how you react at the sight of a giant fireball in your kitchen. The results can be pretty random.

Bill, on the other hand, had come to his senses and had run out the front door and to the elderly neighbor's house and banged on their door frantically. When they finally came to the door he asked as calmly as he was able if he could borrow a fire extinguisher. When they asked him why, he apparently found a final shred of dignity and decided he didn't want to share his part of the catastrophe with total strangers, so he ran back into our house. To this day I wonder about the story those neighbors tell about the panicked young man who didn't know why he needed a fire extinguisher.

We found out later that Bob eventually went back down all three flights of stairs from the attic to the basement only to find that there was no master shut-off for the gas line, which surely breaks several city ordinances and building codes. But he did eventually find an emergency shut-off switch for the pipe. Where did he find it, you ask? Well, at the base of that gas pipe coming up through the floor in the kitchen, of course. That's right, the pipe that currently had a 2,000 degree natural gas torch burning right above it.

To Bob's credit, he quickly grabbed the only tool he could find, a large pipe wrench, and reached under the giant fireball to flip off the emergency switch. And just like that, our friendly fireball visitor was no more. And, likewise, my days of working with gas lines and electricity had come to a safe and very grateful end.

I learned from our little misadventure that you can never be too far away from a house when it explodes, that you always have to go back for your brother (whether you want to or not), and to — always, always — just hire an electrician.

And one last thing — don't judge us too harshly. Your day will come soon enough, and you don't know how you will react. Good luck, much love, and may all your fireballs be extinguished quickly and safely.

Living Large

(airport)

Gate Attendant, looking down at computer terminal: "Yes?"

Me: "I was just wondering ... I know you're busy, but if it's not too much trouble ... I'm in seat 21B, and the row is totally full ... but it looks like row 24 has two open seats next to each other, so I was ..."

Attendant: (still looking down) "Sir, we don't change seat assignments at the gate."

Me: "Well, I was just checking because ..."

Attendant: (still looking down) "Sir. I can't help you."

(long pause)

Me: "I'm a *really* big guy."

Attendant: (looks up)

Attendant: (looks up farther)

Attendant: (slow blink)

Attendant: "So ... that was row 24, you say?"

--- ■ ■ ■ ---

(grocery checkout)

White-haired Cashier Lady: "What is Chaotic Neutral?"

Me: "Huh? Oh, right, I forgot it says 'Chaotic Neutral' on my shirt. It's an inside gamer joke about the philosophy around RPG alignments."

Cashier Lady: "Sounds like a death metal band."

Me: "Yeah, it really does."

Cashier Lady: "I like death metal. Last night it was Goatwhore. And alcohol. It always starts with alcohol."

Me: "Not the conversation I expected to have at Kroger."

Cashier Lady: "I get that a lot."

Me: "I'm not complaining."

--- ∎ ∎ ∎ ---

(restaurant)

Tiny Boy, maybe age three: "Mommy, he's really tall! Look, Mommy! He's really tall!"

His Mom: "Yes, he is. Now let's concentrate on your food."

Tiny Boy: "He's really tall. He's really tall. Is he a giant? Is he a giant?"

His Mom: "I'm so sorry, sir."

Me: "No, I'm not a giant. But when I was little, I ate lots of veggies and they made me extra big and strong. Do you eat vegetables?"

Tiny Boy: (nods, eyes wide)

Me: "Good. Eat your veggies and you'll grow up big and strong like me."

Tiny Boy: "I will."

--- ■ ■ ■ ■ ---

(dials phone)

Hostess: "Good evening, this is Fancy Restaurant. How may I help you?"

Me: "Hi. I was there earlier this evening and I'm wondering if I may have accidentally left an item there."

Hostess: "Oh, I'm so sorry for your inconvenience, sir. I'll be happy to assist you in any way I can. Do you remember the name of your server?"

Me: "Sorry, I'm not sure. Maybe it was … Amy?"

Hostess: "Hmm … Could it have been Teresa?"

Me: "Possibly."

Hostess: "Maybe it was Sarah?"

Me: "Maybe, I guess. I'm really not sure. But, you know, she'll probably remember me. I was the 6'4" Viking wearing a kilt."

(laughter)

Hostess: "Oh yes ... we all remember you."

(more laughter)

--- ■ ■ ■ ■ ---

(in public)

Tiny Girl, maybe five years old: "Hey, you!"

Me: "Yes?"

Tiny Girl: "You are REALLY big!"

Me: "I know! I'm sort of a giant. But the friendly kind of giant, not the mean kind."

Tiny Girl: "And weird."

Me: (blank stare)

--- ■ ■ ■ ■ ---

(drive-thru window)

Window Guy: "That will be $8.57 please."

Me: "Here's my debit card."

Window Guy: "Hey … know who you look like?"

Me: "I have a guess."

Window Guy: "Yeah … The Dude. You look just like The Dude, man."

Me: "Yes. Strong similarity."

Window Guy: "Cool. I bet you get that a lot."

Me: "I do, actually. Very often. Especially when I'm wearing a bathrobe."

Window Guy: "Haha! Bathrobe, right. Hilarious."

Me: "Thanks."

Window Guy: "You're really cool about it."

Me: "I think it's cool."

Window Guy: "Cool."

(long pause)

Me: "Can I have my food?"

Window Guy: "Oh … yeah."

--- ■ ■ ■ ■ ---

Tiny Boy: "I'm holding the door for you."

Me: "Yes, and thank you very much, little man."

Tiny Boy: "You are welcome, big hairy guy."

--- ■ ■ ■ ■ ---

Young Hostess: "How many in your party tonight?"

Me: "Just me, but I promise to eat a lot."

Hostess: "Oh, I'm sure."

Me: (chuckle)

Hostess: (eyes wide) "I'm so sorry! I didn't mean it like … I wasn't saying that you're …"

Me: "It's OK. I thought it was funny."

Hostess: "Oh, thank God. Some people are really sensitive about stuff like that."

Me: "It's all good. I'm not sensitive like that."

Hostess: "Good. You don't look sensitive at all."

Me: "Well, it's good to know I don't look sensitive."

Hostess: "Oh God! I did it again! I didn't mean it like that."

Me: "It's totally cool. I didn't take it that way."

(long pause)

Me: "Can I have a table?"

Hostess: "Oh, right. Follow me."

--- ■ ■ ■ ---

Little Old Lady, leaning into my face: "You are a *really* big guy."

Me: "Yes, ma'am. I am."

Little Old Lady: "I bet it's great looking down at everybody."

Me: "Well, no one messes with me, that's true."

Little Old Lady: "I wouldn't take any crap from anybody."

Little Old Lady: (punches at the air) "Pow! Pow! Pow!"

--- ■ ■ ■ ---

(works for ten hours straight)

Me: "I'm having a bad day."

(thermostat broken at work, temps at desk hit over 80 degrees)

Me: "I'm having a horrible day."

(didn't have time, completely skipped dinner)

Me: "I'm having a horrible, horrible day."

(watches the Lifeline helicopter take off from the hospital helipad next to my parking garage)

Me: (slow blink)

Me: "You know, I'm having a pretty good day."

The Age of Diners

I feel almost guilty for sneaking out at 10 am on a weekday for a quick breakfast and a grocery trip, but then the diner's parking lot is surprisingly almost full.

I walk inside and the place is bustling. I must not be the only one with some freedom in my schedule. I notice I'm the only patron here that doesn't have a full head of white hair. I guess I'm out of my age bracket this morning.

I'm certainly the youngest customer here, except the four-year-old girl squealing two booths over.

Her grandma is shushing her dutifully, but you can tell her heart isn't in it. Grandma loves those squeals and doesn't mind everyone hearing them.

To be honest, I'm kind of enjoying it myself. Squealer is having more fun than anyone else. Hey, I get it. Going out for breakfast with your grandma is magical.

I wish there were more old diners still around. They're a dying breed. It's unfair that they've almost all been replaced with fast food places and corporate chains. I don't think my kids really get the distinction. I saddens me to think they can feel the difference in the vibe.

Why does the modern dining experience have to feel so manufactured now? So predictable? What's wrong with serving simple food the way it used to be, the way it always was? I know it's a business and they have to make money, but I want more options in that wide, delicious middle ground between the clown's drive-thru and some hip Mediterranean Fusion Gastro Pub.

The guy behind me is talking too loud. I wish he had more to say. If I'm being forced to hear it, I think I deserve more than just day-to-day drivel. I haven't heard anyone else at his table, so they must be speaking at normal volume. Loud Dude's phone rings and he takes the call, of course, on speakerphone, of course, with the volume way too loud. It occurs to me that Loud Dude is probably losing his hearing, and I feel a little bad for him. A little.

My food arrives. My waitress is younger than me, probably mid-twenties, but her eyes look tired. She's quick to refill my coffee cup each time she passes. She looks like she probably has kids and a husband who works long hours with his hands. Something in her eyes tells me she didn't get enough sleep last night, or most nights, but she still has a little bounce to her step. She seems genuinely nice. Her smile is big and friendly and I hope she makes enough money today. I'm sure she earns every penny of it. I've waited tables, I know how grueling it is. Slinging food is honest work, but it won't make you rich. I decide to tip her too much.

My "deluxe" omelet is filled with generous hunks of meat of questionable origin. The bacon looks like the paper thin pre-cooked type, as does the diced sausage patties. The ham is clearly just lunch meat. I'm reminded that, at least in theory, I'm trying to eat higher quality and less quantity. But the processed American cheese has melted into a bright, yellow-orange goo that tastes like my childhood. Also, the grilled onions and green peppers are fresh and real. That makes it healthy, I tell myself.

Grandma keeps calling the girl "Sissy." That must mean she has siblings. I wonder if they're older or younger. Maybe her mom is in the hospital having her baby brother or sister right now. I can't see if she's wearing the obligatory "Big Sister" T-shirt. Regardless, it's an odd nickname, Sissy. It doesn't impart much info, and it's definitely still a playground insult, isn't it?

I decide I don't like the nickname "Sissy." Though, to be fair, my referring to her as "Squealer" isn't any better. But at least I have the excuse of not knowing her real name.

I remember taking the boy out to eat when his little sister was born. He wore his "I'm the Big Brother" shirt with beaming pride. I got him whatever he wanted for a couple weeks. I don't remember when my little brother was born. But I don't have to — it's always been pretty clear that older siblings need lots of extra attention for a while after a new baby comes along. Little siblings are cute, but they sure do hog all the attention. It's not easy going from the center of it all to second fiddle overnight, especially when you're only three.

I can barely hear the twang of the piped-in country music over the hum of the crowd and Loud Dude. I can tell it's "new country," so I probably wouldn't recognize it anyway. They've never had country music playing here before today. I wonder how they choose the music each day. Maybe it's a rotation of some sort. A million years ago when I worked in restaurants, choosing the music was a privilege reserved for the manager on duty. Maybe there's a new manager.

The table next to me is laughing a lot. It's two couples, all clearly retired and old friends. They looked to have been done eating long before I got here, and they're in no hurry. I don't doubt they will be here long after I've gone back to work. Suddenly I'm looking forward to being retired.

I'm curious what's so funny because they're really cracking up. I wish I was having that much fun. Even without being able to make out their conversation, it's pleasant just to see and hear them enjoying themselves so much. Laughing is healthy.

A plate breaks with a loud crash back in the kitchen. There's scattered applause and snickering across the crowd and then an awkward hush. I grin at the spectacle and it feels like we're all friends that experienced something together.

It always feels odd to me to feel the natural pull of group dynamics. It's written in our DNA to seek out and identify with groups of people. I still feel a little out of place here because of my age, and I've gotten more than a few sideways looks at my long beard and wild hair. But I'm still part of the group. We're all here, in this moment.

Time seems to pass more slowly in an old diner. I think that's why I love them so much.

I stand up and put a ten dollar bill on the table. It's an obnoxious tip, but she deserves it. Hopefully, it will make a difference. If nothing else, maybe it will cheer her up a little. I like the idea that it might encourage her to keep working hard toward her dreams. Maybe she will use it for a special indulgence just for herself, as a reward for putting in a long day on her feet after whatever kept her up last night. But knowing young mothers, she'll most likely share it with her family.

It wasn't on the menu, but I walk out with a sense of calm and belonging that I didn't have when I entered. I shared food with people. I broke bread among friends. Well, sort of friends. I could have chosen to talk with any of them and they would have been friendly.

Of course, it probably won't feel so friendly later when all this grease upsets my stomach. I'm not so young anymore, you know.

The Wonderful Wife

Wonderful Wife: "What do you want to do for Father's Day?"

Me: "Nothing, really. I'm fine. We don't need to do anything."

Wonderful Wife: "Well, I thought you'd like to at least hit a brunch. There's got to be some all-you-can-eat bacon with your name on it somewhere."

Me: (slow blink)

Me: "I have never loved you more than I do at this very moment."

--- ■ ■ ■ ---

(setting up workstation in vacation house)

Me: "Oh, CRAP."

Wonderful Wife: "What's wrong dear?"

Me: "CRAP. CRAP. CRAP. CRAP. CRAP."

Wonderful Wife: "Is there a problem?"

Me: "I have to set up my work laptop so I can work while you guys are at the beach, but I can't connect to Wi-Fi, and I have to figure this out or drive home or it will ruin our vacation, or maybe I'll setup outside, or find a Starbucks, but that really messes up my plans, and this is just not working out, and I think I'm going to lose my …"

Wonderful Wife: "Or … you could just use the hard-wired internet connection right here with this LAN cable hanging out of it."

(long pause)

Me: "OK. That could work."

--- ∎ ∎ ∎ ---

Me: "Hey, wanna go out for dinner tonight?"

Wonderful Wife: "I really don't feel well. I have a horrible headache and the lymph nodes in my neck are swollen."

Me: (typing on my phone)

Me: "I looked up your symptoms. I'm afraid you only have a few hours to live."

Wonderful Wife: (heads into kitchen)

Me: "What are you doing?"

Wonderful Wife: "Making Pop-Tarts and chocolate Nesquik. If I'm going to die, that's how I'm going out."

--- ■ ■ ■ ---

Wonderful Wife: "What's for dinner?"

Me: "I want to eat out, but I'm too tired to go anywhere. Let's have food delivered."

Wonderful Wife: "Sure thing. Like what?"

Me: "I want food delivered."

Wonderful Wife: "Yes, but what *type* of food."

Me: "I want the type of food that magically appears in front of me."

Wonderful Wife: "So, anything?"

Me: "I'm too tired to even choose."

Wonderful Wife: "Wow. Do you plan to at least chew it yourself?"

Me: "I'll struggle through it."

Wonderful Wife: "You're an inspiration to us all."

Me: "You're welcome."

--- ■ ■ ■ ---

Me: "Maybe I'll become a Buddhist. In a lot of ways I'm already pretty close to a Buddhist."

Wonderful Wife: "Yeah, your belly already looks like Buddha."

Me: ...

--- ■ ■ ■ ---

Wonderful Wife: "I'm sick."

Me: "I'm feeling terrible myself."

Wonderful Wife: "Nope. We can't both be sick. I called it first. Suck it up, buddy."

(long pause)

Me: "You know, I feel better already."

--- ∎ ∎ ∎ ---

Me: "Why are you wearing the pajama pants that you gave to me for Christmas?"

Wonderful Wife: "The question is, now that flannel fleece was invented, why are they still making clothes out of other fabrics?"

With Child

Sometimes you grow up and get to have a child.

And they are so tiny when you catch them, slippery and bloodied, straight from The Mama, who's been pushing and screaming and crying for hours, as well as waddling for months and peeing around the clock and eating weird stuff.

The Mama's being so brave and, sure, you've been there for her, you guess. Maybe. But you know it's all about The Mama, because it's really obvious she's doing The Hard Part and you're just some geek trying to be the provider and protector that Nature intended. Except, you're not sure you're very good at providing or protecting, so you try to hold the door for her sometimes and maybe you're funny sometimes and you try to make her happy.

But now she's made you a baby, a tiny copy of you that will carry on your good parts and your bad parts and your last name. And you can't make babies, so it's the most gracious and amazing and mind-blowing gift that you can't possibly ever repay. That's why it's all about The Mama, and will always be all about The Mama, because you're just The Dad and maybe you'll teach the kid to play baseball or chess or something someday.

But, at that moment, right when she's freshly arrived, for a few seconds it's just you and this tiny new person, and suddenly you have The Entire Future of Mankind in those big, clumsy hands of yours. Time kind of stops and the room empties and it's just you, holding your child. She's, at once, the most beautiful and terrifying thing you've ever seen, and O-M-G you are now The Man. In a blink of her tiny eye you are changed forever, and you know somehow your life has a purpose and no more excuses buddy and this small, helpless human is counting on you so don't screw it up.

But for that time, right then, you look there in your hands, and she's so new and so pink and so angry, and wow look at those tiny fingers, and she totally looks like you, and she's screaming and healthy and everything is just so very perfect.

And a tiny voice, deep, deep inside you says, "It will never get any better than this."

Carried Away

Someone likes to pretend she's asleep in the car when we get home.

Someone likes to be carried up to bed.

Someone thinks Dad can't tell she's faking.

Someone thinks she's a pretty good faker.

But Dad knows.

He knows she gets heavier every time.

He knows any day now she'll be too big, too grown up to be carried.

Dad plays along and carries her, heavy, up all those stairs.

Every step, he wonders if this is the last time he'll get to carry his tiny girl.

She thinks she's getting away with something.

He feels her getting away.

Little Miss Thing

Me: "Go back to bed"

Little Miss Thing, age three: "The Big Bad Wolf will get me."

Me: "There is no such thing as the Big Bad Wolf. It's just in stories. Go back to bed."

Little Miss Thing: "Yes, there is."

Me: "OK, look. Your daddy is bigger and badder than the Big Bad Wolf, and I told him to stay away from our house."

Little Miss Thing: (long pause) "OK. I will throw sticks at him if I see him. Good night."

(pads off to bed)

--- ■ ■ ■ ---

Danger Monkey, age six: "She's not really asleep, Dad."

Little Miss Thing, age three: (yelling) "I'M ASLEEP!"

Me: "You know, kiddo ... As a general rule, people who scream 'I'm asleep' are not really asleep."

Little Miss Thing: (whispering) *"I'm asleep."*

--- ■ ■ ■ ---

Little Miss Thing, age four, stepping out of tub: "Done with my bath."

Me: "No, you haven't washed your hair yet."

Little Miss Thing: "Yes, I did! I washed my hair!"

Me: "Then why is it dry?"

Little Miss Thing: (pause)

Little Miss Thing: "It just dried very quickly tonight."

--- ■ ■ ■ ---

Little Miss Thing, age four: "Want to see my cool dance moves?"

Me: "Yes, of course!"

(she flails around randomly)

Me: "That was great dancing."

Little Miss Thing: "I know. I dance a lot."

--- ■ ■ ■ ---

Little Miss Thing, age four: "Can I have a cookie for breakfast?"

Me: "No, of course not."

Little Miss Thing: "Can I have ... three?"

Me: "Absolutely not."

Little Miss Thing: "Can I have ... one hundred and one?"

Me: "You are either horrible at negotiating, or brilliant at it. I can't tell yet."

--- ■ ■ ■ ---

Little Miss Thing, age four: "Daddy, read this book to me."

Me: "Oh, my. Well, you see ... this here is your mother's copy of *Where the Wild Things Are* from when she was your age. How cool is that? And, look here! That handwriting right there is an inscription from Grandma and ..."

Little Miss Thing: "Just read the book."

--- ■ ■ ■ ■ ---

Wonderful Wife: "Please go upstairs and *POLITELY* and *GENTLY* inform your brother that I say it's time for him to finish his shower."

Little Miss Thing, age five, literally kicks open the bathroom door: "Hey, you! Turn off the water and get out! It's my turn!"

(long pause)

Me: "I think she nailed it."

--- ■ ■ ■ ■ ---

Me: "Your pajamas are on backwards."

Little Miss Thing, age five: "No they aren't."

Me: "Yes, they are. Don't lie. I can clearly see the tag sticking out under your chin."

Little Miss Thing: "These aren't my pajamas."

(slow blink)

Me: "You win."

--- ■ ■ ■ ■ ---

Little Miss Thing, age five: "Daddy, do you want my apple?"

Me: "Sure. Wait a minute — why does this apple have a wooden stick in it?"

Little Miss Thing: "It used to be a caramel apple. I only like the caramel."

(long pause)

Me: "On second thought, I'm going to pass."

--- ■ ■ ■ ■ ---

Little Miss Thing, age five: "I'll just swim in shorts."

My Oldest, age fourteen: "No, sorry. Girls have to wear tops."

Little Miss Thing: "Why? Boys don't wear tops."

My Oldest: "Boys are allowed. Girls aren't."

Little Miss Thing: "Why?"

My Oldest: "The Patriarchy says so. Which is just another reason to fight the Patriarchy."

Little Miss Thing: "Where is the Patriarchy? I want to talk to them."

--- ■ ■ ■ ---

Little Miss Thing, age six: "Does the jelly go in the fridge, or in the cabinet?"

Me: "Does the label say 'refrigerate after opening'?"

Little Miss Thing: (reading) "Yes."

Me: "Then follow the instructions."

(20 minutes later)

Me: "Why is this jelly jar in the fridge with the lid off???"

Little Miss Thing: "The label says to put it in the fridge with the lid off."

Me: "It says … what now?"

Little Miss Thing: (pointing to label) "See … 'Refrigerate after opening'."

(slow blink)

Me: "You know, actually, you're totally right."

--- ■ ■ ■ ---

(arguing is heard upstairs)

Danger Monkey, age nine: "It's a free country!"

Little Miss Thing, age six: "But it's my bedroom!"

Danger Monkey: "It's a free country!"

Little Miss Thing: "But it's my bedroom!"

Me: (shouting) "Hey! You two upstairs! I don't care what you're arguing about, but you need to use your brains and your words to come to a creative solution. Learn to compromise. Don't just shout the same things over and over."

Danger Monkey: (whisper) *"What did he say?"*

Little Miss Thing: (whisper) *"He said you're kicked out of my room for the rest of the day."*

Danger Monkey: "Awww, man!"

--- ∎ ∎ ∎ ---

Little Miss Thing, age six: "Daddy, bring me a plate."

Me: "I think you need to find a better way to ask than that."

Little Miss Thing: "Plates don't have legs — it isn't going to walk out here by itself!"

Me: "Try again."

Little Miss Thing: "Please bring me a plate?"

Me: "There you go."

--- ∎ ∎ ∎ ---

Little Miss Thing, age six: "I want to be an adult."

Me: "There's no hurry, honey. Being an adult is not as much fun as it seems."

Little Miss Thing: "Yes it is! Adults get to drive and go on dates, and they make their kids do everything while they just sit and watch TV."

Me: "You got me. Being an adult really is cool."

--- ■ ■ ■ ---

Me: "I made the dinner, so you kids need to clean up the dishes."

Little Miss Thing, age six: "I can't."

Me: "And why not?"

Little Miss Thing: "It's bad for my self-esteem."

Me: "I think I'll take that risk."

--- ■ ■ ■ ---

Wonderful Wife: "I'm exhausted. I just want to sleep for a week."

Little Miss Thing, age six: "I can do your hair while you sleep."

Wonderful Wife: "That sounds nice, actually."

Little Miss Thing: "Where's the shaving cream?"

(long pause)

Wonderful Wife: "I will never sleep again."

--- ■ ■ ■ ---

(small town festival)

Vendor Guy: "Everybody's a winner! Spin the wheel, get a prize! Congratulations little lady … your spin landed on red. You can choose any item from that table."

Little Miss Thing, age six: "Anything? Really?"

Vendor: "You bet, sweetie! Anything on the table."

(long pause)

Little Miss Thing: "I want that." (points at iPad)

Vendor: "No, not my iPad."

Little Miss Thing: "You said anything on the table."

Vendor: "Well, yeah ... but ... I meant ... anything except the iPad."

Little Miss Thing: (long stare)

Little Miss Thing: "Then never mind."

(walks away)

--- ■ ■ ■ ■ ---

Little Miss Thing, age seven: "Can I learn how to unlock your car?"

Me: "Sure, kiddo. Here's the key."

Little Miss Thing: "How do I unlock everything all at once?"

Me: "Sadly, I bought this car used and it doesn't work that way. The guy said you have to unlock the driver door, then reach inside to unlock."

Little Miss Thing: "I think you turn it and hold it." (turns key and holds)

Me: "No, don't keep it turned like that. It ..."

(all locks on car pop unlocked)

Me: (slow blink)

Little Miss Thing: "Told ya."

Me: …

--- ∎ ∎ ∎ ∎ ---

Little Miss Thing, age seven, walks up shuffling a deck of cards: "Daddy, pick a card."

Me: "Hmmm … Let me see. I choose this one."

Little Miss Thing: (shuffles then flips them over)

Little Miss Thing: "Sorry, you lose." (walks away)

Me: …

--- ∎ ∎ ∎ ∎ ---

Me: "What are you thinking of giving your little sister for Christmas?"

My Oldest, age fifteen: "It's hard to choose. I really want to get her a future career dress-up kit, but there's no kit for 'World Domination.' I guess I'll just go with veterinarian."

--- ∎ ∎ ∎ ∎ ---

Me: "Time for lights out."

Little Miss Thing, age seven: (keeps reading)

Me: "I can see you in your bed reading."

Little Miss Thing: (keeps reading)

Me: "Lights out. For real."

Little Miss Thing: (keeps reading)

Me: "Time for sleep. Book down. Go to sleep."

Little Miss Thing: (keeps reading)

Me: "It would be nice to be acknowledged."

Little Miss Thing: "You know what would be nice? Reading uninterrupted."

Me: …

Me: (turns off the light, heads downstairs)

Me: "Goodnight, kiddo."

Little Miss Thing: "You're mean!"

Me: "I love you, too."

--- ■ ■ ■ ---

Little Miss Thing, age seven: "Pass me the milk."

Me: "What's the magic word?"

Little Miss Thing: "NOW!"

Me: "Uh … No. That's definitely not it."

Little Miss Thing: "Are you sure? It works sometimes."

--- ■ ■ ■ ---

Little Miss Thing, age seven: "Are we there yet?"

Me: "Almost. Maybe an hour."

Little Miss Thing: "I'm bored."

Wonderful Wife: "There's an app on my phone that will teach you Spanish."

Little Miss Thing: "I don't want to learn Spanish. I'm bored."

Wonderful Wife: "Probably best. If you learned Spanish, you and your sister could tell secrets."

Me: "Yeah, you better not learn Spanish. You two could say things like 'Daddy's feet stink' in Spanish and I wouldn't even know it."

Little Miss Thing: "Give me that!" (evil laughter)

(30 minutes later)

Little Miss Thing: "I'm now 3 percent fluent in Spanish. Soy una niña. That means 'I'm a girl'."

Me: "Yep. You sure tricked us. Better not learn any more Spanish."

Little Miss Thing: (evil laughter)

--- ■ ■ ■ ---

Me: "I love you. You are strong, smart, and beautiful."

Little Miss Thing, age seven: "Good. You too."

Me: "Thank you. I'm very proud of you."

Little Miss Thing: "Yeah, I know."

Me: "Good."

(long pause)

Little Miss Thing: "My favorite dessert is cheesecake. I thought you should know that."

Me: "Noted."

--- ■ ■ ■ ---

Little Miss Thing, age seven: "Grandma, look! I'm wearing heels!"

My Mother: "Very nice. How is your balance?"

(Little Miss Thing falls)

My Mother: "Oh no! Are you OK?"

Little Miss Thing: "I fell on my butt."

My Mother: "Oh my! Did you hurt your bottom?"

Little Miss Thing: "It's OK. It already had a crack in it."

My Mother: (stunned silence)

--- ■ ■ ■ ---

Me: "What? Why are you downstairs? I tucked you in fifteen minutes ago."

Little Miss Thing, age seven: "You did it wrong."

Me: "Excuse me?"

Little Miss Thing: (produces book)

Me: "What? The American Girl's *Babysitters Handbook*?"

Little Miss Thing: "Page 61. It says when you tuck in children, you should sit and read to them."

Me: "Well, that's more of a suggest ..."

Little Miss Thing: (running up stairs) "I already have a book picked out for you."

(long pause)

Wonderful Wife: "She did provide documentation."

Me: "I blame you."

--- ■ ■ ■ ---

(school office 9 am)

Little Miss Thing, age seven: "You have to fill out a tardy slip for me."

Me: "OK, I seem to remember that from last time."

Little Miss Thing: "You should check 'Overslept' for the reason."

Me: "Sure."

Little Miss Thing: (loudly) "He overslept, not me. I was ready and made my own breakfast."

School Secretary: "Good for you, kiddo."

Little Miss Thing: "I had to wake him up. I think he's sick."

Me: "She doesn't need all the ugly details."

School Secretary: "I've heard a lot worse than that."

Me: "I bet you have."

--- ■ ■ ■ ---

Me: "What's wrong, kiddo? Why aren't you in bed?"

Little Miss Thing, age seven: "I HATE lightning storms!" (shakes fist)

(lightning flashes)

Little Miss Thing: (eyes wide) "That lightning happened right when I punched. Do you think I made it happen?"

Me: "Pretty sure that wasn't you."

Little Miss Thing: "Let's check."

(furiously shaking fist)

(no lightning)

Little Miss Thing: "OK, I checked. I guess I'm not Mother Nature after all."

--- ■ ■ ■ ---

(at county fair)

Me: "Here, you can help me by shaking some salt on Mom's corn on the cob."

Little Miss Thing, age seven: "I'm a good shaker."

Me: "Yes, you have mad skills. Now salt the other side."

Little Miss Thing: "NO! DON'T TURN IT OVER!"

Me: "Honey, I have to turn it over so you can shake salt on the underside, too."

Little Miss Thing: "I can do it."

Me: "No, you can't shake salt up."

Little Miss Thing: "I can do it. Watch."

(violent shaking in upward motion)

(seventeen grains of salt eventually hit the corn)

Little Miss Thing: "I told you."

Me: "I should have never doubted you."

--- ■ ■ ■ ---

Wonderful Wife: "You need to be totally ready for the bus in five minutes. You don't want to miss the bus on the first day of school."

Little Miss Thing, age seven: "But, I AM totally ready."

Wife: "No, you're not. Now go finish getting ready."

Little Miss Thing: "I AM READY!"

(long pause)

Wonderful Wife: "I recommend shoes and socks."

Little Miss Thing: (looks at bare feet)

Little Miss Thing: "Oh, yeah."

(runs off)

--- ■ ■ ■ ---

Me: "Time for tuck-in."

Little Miss Thing, age seven: "You have to tell me a story."

Me: "I don't think we have time tonight, kiddo. It's very late and ..."

Little Miss Thing: "YOU HAVE TO."

Me: "Come on, now. I'm sure you can get to sleep without a story. It's super late and we've had a big, big day. Extra snuggles and a squeeze for you. There we go. Nighty-night, Honey."

(long pause)

Little Miss Thing: "I'll wake up Mom if I have to."

(long pause)

Me: "How about Three Little Pigs?"

Gone, Baby, Gone

Two little dolls made me cry today.

Little Miss Thing is having a birthday party tomorrow. The big seven. She's a sassy 2nd grader, enjoying all the perks of being a Big Kid. She's reading the Harry Potter books. She's losing teeth every couple of weeks. She's developed a keen fashion sense. Mostly she doesn't ask for help reaching the kitchen cabinets anymore, which makes her feel grown up.

We have the kids clean out their rooms right before birthdays, giving their older toys to Goodwill. We like that it keeps down the clutter. The kids like that their old, forgotten toys move on to new kids who will love them. It's always a difficult process, but they choose very carefully. Who better to know which toys have passed their prime?

Flashback to two years ago this week, when we were in Florida at Disney World. Our kindergartner turned five in the most magical place on Earth.

It was a whirlwind of glitter and musical numbers and she couldn't stop smiling. We have pictures of her dressed as Anna from *Frozen*, holding an Anna doll while meeting the "real-life" Anna and Elsa. She got the *Frozen* slippers, *Frozen* alarm clock, *Frozen* pajamas, *Frozen* nightlight, and *Frozen* toothbrush ... the whole setup. She got the movie and the soundtrack, and memorized them both immediately.

But most of all she wanted the Anna and Elsa dolls. They were sisters, she reasoned. They should be together. They rarely left her side, literally sleeping with them for months. Every morning was a fight to keep her from taking them to school. More than once I caught them being smuggled in her backpack. A couple times she got them past us.

When you're a parent, it is super rare to feel like you're doing anything right. Everything is made up as you go, and full of last-minute compromises, if not totally half baked. You always are making do with what you have. You never have enough energy or time to do all the things. You can't make all the meals, and check all the homework, and clean the whole house, and sing all the songs at tuck-ins, and make all the costumes, and kiss all the booboos, and right all the wrongs. You just can't.

But every once in a while, you hit a sweet spot. If you keep at it, eventually things will line up. You're never sure if it was truly you that made it happen, or if it was The Universe or God or pure dumb luck. But, you take it. You claim it as your own, and for that one single moment you get to feel like a real parent. You get to feel like you can do this. Like your kids aren't going to be screwed up like you are. You hope. Maybe.

Little Miss Thing on her birthday at Disney World was one of those rare times when I felt like a good dad. Yes, it was stupid commercialized plastic crap that cost too much. Yes, it was scripted by marketers. Yes, it's basically a scam.

But, dammit, she was happy. Really, really happy. The smile on her face was big and goofy and new. Those two over-priced, imported, big-eyed dolls made my baby girl very, very happy, and that was good enough for me.

So, this morning when those dolls showed up on the pile for Goodwill, some tears may have come out of my eyes. Gently squirted. Lightly dribbled. Briefly sprayed. I mean, I didn't weep or blubber or anything. Well, maybe a little.

What's odd is the same thing happened with the older kids, but I didn't cry about it. With My Oldest, it was *Dora the Explorer*. For her fourth birthday she got the whole Dora miniature play set. It had a fridge and stove and wardrobe and her Abuela and an optional swimming pool. That girl must have danced those tiny Dora and Boots dolls for ten hours straight that first day. And probably every day after, for months. Those lumps of colored plastic made her very happy, and that made me happy. And, then, a couple years passed in a blink of an eye and Dora, her Abuela, and the optional pool were all on the pile.

For the boy, it was *Thomas the Tank Engine*. That kid knew every name of every train. He knew who was nice, who was mean, who worked hard and who pulled pranks. He knew the tractor, and the bus, and helicopter and the people who drove them. I remember how he would patiently correct me when I confused Percy for James, his tiny voice full of pity for my incompetence. He deeply loved all his Thomas DVDs and his train play table and Thomas blanket and Thomas sheets on his big-boy bed. They made him happy. And then, in a hot blink, they all showed up on the pile.

I guess today hit me hard because our little one is not so little anymore. She doesn't need us like she used to. Even as irritating and time consuming and messy and loud and smelly as it can be, the truth is that — being needed by your kids is kind of nice. You know your place, and you know you matter. You matter a lot.

I think maybe it's different this time because she's our last. Today's *Frozen* purge means that our baby isn't really a baby anymore. Ready or not, that chapter of our lives has ended. And, sure, you won't catch me complaining that diapers are a thing of the past. But it hurts a little to not be as important as I used to be.

As a parent, I know it's my job to make sure that eventually they won't need me. It's a job I take very seriously. They're great kids, growing up strong and smart and funny and kind. I'm proud of all three of them. My heart swells to see my babies become such cool young people, and I get some wonderful glimpses of the awesome adults they will become. But none of that means it

doesn't catch me right in the tear ducts
sometimes.

This is all just the way these things work, of
course. It's all part of the big circle of life that's
been happening since we pulled ourselves out of
caves and stood upright.

I guess I'm just sad knowing that, soon enough, in
a quick blink, I'll be on that pile myself.

It's a Boy!

A few years ago I met a little blond boy who wasn't quite one year old yet. He was wearing tiny, yellow footie pajamas and playing with some blocks and a tractor on his living room floor. He didn't even look up when I walked in.

I had just walked his mom home after our second date. Being the suave bachelor, I had a rule that we weren't supposed to meet each other's kids until things were serious. But, life gets messy and being a single parent is complicated, so this particular night it was just easier to have the sitter stay at the house.

So, when we got back from dinner, there he was. I mean, seeing as he lived there and all. I paid the sitter (because it seemed like the nice thing to do) and then The Mom and I sat on separate couches and chatted for a bit while he played on the floor between us. She made sure to officially introduce us, but clearly he was a lot more interested in the tractor. I don't blame him. It was a pretty cool tractor.

After a bit, The Mom announced it was bedtime. He stood up, walked over with his arms wide, and gave me a hug. A real hug. A big squeezey number. The little dude snuggled right up on me like we'd known each other forever.

I patted him gently on his fuzzy little back and said, "I don't think we're supposed to be bonding yet, buddy." But there I was, fifteen minutes after meeting him, and I felt like he was already my kid.

With that said, I want the world to know that I officially adopted The Danger Monkey not too long after his tenth birthday. By all rights and legal standing, he is now my son.

No more writing "step-dad" on forms. No more explaining to well-meaning folks that I'm not his "real father." Now, I'm just his dad.

Simple as that.

Other than those formalities, not much changed. He's called me Dad for a long time. As far as he can remember, I've always been around. And I've always treated him as my own. Because he is my own. I couldn't love him any more than I already do. I couldn't be any prouder of him.

So, in the end, legal status is important and I'm really glad that the State of Indiana, the IRS, and our insurance company recognize me as his father. Which is nice.

But, you see, the thing is — he and I had that cleared up a long time ago.

The Danger Monkey

Danger Monkey, age seven: "Look … I'm dead."

(flops over and lies still for a full minute)

Danger Monkey: "Was that a good dead impersonation?"

Me: "Yes. But for the record, most dead bodies are not smiling mischievously."

--- ■ ■ ■ ---

Wonderful Wife: "We're going swimming at the Lake!"

Me: "Better be careful of the sharks."

Other kids: "SHARKS!?"

Danger Monkey, age seven: "Sharks only live in salt water. This lake is fresh water. There are no sharks."

(long pause)

Me: "Don't make me regret giving you all those science books."

--- ■ ■ ■ ■ ---

Danger Monkey, age seven: "I bet I can pack my lunch in under two minutes."

Me: "No way. You goof around too much. A monkey with a brick glued to his butt could make a lunch faster than you do."

Danger Monkey: "Yeah, but he has four hands with opposable thumbs."

Me: (slow blink)

Me: "OK. You win."

--- ■ ■ ■ ■ ---

Restaurant Hostess: "Just two tonight? And how old is your daughter?"

Danger Monkey, age nine: "I'm nine ... and, if it matters, I'm a boy."

Hostess: "Oh, I am so sorry!"

Danger Monkey: "It's OK. Is it the same price?"

Hostess: "What?"

Danger Monkey: "Do you charge the same price for boys and girls?"

Hostess: "Oh, of course."

Danger Monkey: "Then it doesn't matter if I'm a boy or a girl."

Hostess: "I guess not."

--- ■ ■ ■ ---

Danger Monkey, age nine: "Hey, Dad!"

Me: "What's up, son?"

Danger Monkey: "You won't believe it! We found a place in the woods that's super soggy like a swamp. And it's covered in these huge briars that scrape your skin really bad. And you have to crawl on your belly in the mud just to get through."

Me: "Then why crawl through it?"

Danger Monkey: "It's our new clubhouse! It's PERFECT!" (runs off)

--- ■ ■ ■ ■ ---

Me: "Glad you're enjoying your long bath. Time to wash your hair."

Danger Monkey, age nine: "No, hair washing comes at the end."

Me: "Yes. This is the end."

Danger Monkey: "It feels more like the middle."

Me: "End."

Danger Monkey: "Now I'll never know how long it takes to turn into a dolphin."

Me: "There's always tomorrow night."

--- ■ ■ ■ ---

Me: "How is your turkey sandwich?"

Danger Monkey, age nine: "It's OK, I guess."

Me: "Yeah, turkey is kind of dull. What would make it better? Mayonnaise? Avocado? Tomato?"

Danger Monkey: "How about … ham … and bacon!"

Me: "You make a Viking dad so proud, son."

--- ■ ■ ■ ---

Me: "Look, kids. The hotel lobby has ice water with cucumber in it. See the little green slices."

Danger Monkey, age nine: "No way! I hate cucumbers."

Me: "Well, I'm only assuming it's cucumber. It could be sliced up snakes."

Danger Monkey: "That's disgusting!"

(pause)

Danger Monkey: "I'll try it."

--- ∎∎∎ ---

(pediatrician's office, two of us in exam room)

Me: "So, this flyer says boys around age ten may start taking unnecessary risks."

Danger Monkey, age ten: "Really?"

(he jumps off exam table onto his face)

Me: "I just can't imagine what they mean."

(he rides rolling exam stool into wall with his face)

Danger Monkey: "I don't know, either."

(he climbs wall, hits face on window sill)

Me: "Yeah, it's a big mystery."

--- ∎∎∎ ---

Me: "Son, there are few things in this life that make a Viking Dad happier than his son learning how to make chili from scratch. I'm so proud."

Danger Monkey, age ten: "I just followed your instructions."

Me: "I helped steer you, yes, but you did all the work. You even diced the onion yourself."

Danger Monkey: "My chili smells really good."

Me: "It will get better the longer you let it simmer. But, as one chili guy to another, I hereby give you the honor of the first taste test."

Danger Monkey: (dips spoon, tastes his chili)

Danger Monkey: "By the Gods of Olympus! That is delicious!"

(long pause)

Danger Monkey: "That means I really liked it."

Me: "Yeah, I know."

Danger Monkey: "Are you crying?"

--- ■ ■ ■ ---

Danger Monkey, age ten: "Dad, why did the Easter Bunny leave the Easter eggs?"

Me: "Actually, it's an interesting history. Easter originated as a pagan holiday that was appropriated from ancient worship of Oestre, the goddess of fertility. Her symbols included rabbits and eggs, which has morphed into the odd concept we know today as the Easter Bunny."

Danger Monkey: "Nope. The correct answer is because the Easter Chicken was too chicken."

Me: (slow blink)

Me: "Oh, so you were making a joke."

Danger Monkey: "Yeah, and you were WAY OFF."

Me: …

--- ▪ ▪ ▪ ---

Danger Monkey, age ten: "This math problem is really frustrating."

Me: "Do you need help?"

Danger Monkey: "No, it's OK. I understand the math, but the story problem is all wrong."

Me: "Those can be tough."

Danger Monkey: "There's just no way fifteen kids chose Fettuccine Alfredo over pizza or tacos."

(long pause)

Me: "I'm so glad I get to be your Dad."

--- ■ ■ ■ ■ ---

Danger Monkey, age ten: "Do you want to play this new role playing game I'm designing?"

Me: "Maybe. I'm kinda busy. Grown-ups don't usually have time to play games."

Danger Monkey: "It takes place before The Big Bang. I call it Dead Sky. You play one of the Angry Gods who are fighting each other and eventually destroy their world, which then becomes The Universe as we know it."

Me: "Dude ... I am so in."

--- ■ ■ ■ ■ ---

My Oldest, age sixteen: (singing)

Danger Monkey, age ten: "That song's annoying. Stop singing."

My Oldest: (sings louder)

Danger Monkey: "OK, you lose ten points."

My Oldest: "What points?"

Danger Monkey: "You just lost ten points for your House."

My Oldest: "I don't care."

Danger Monkey: "Minus ten more points for not caring."

My Oldest: (rolls eyes)

Me: "You know, son, we're all in the same house. Taking away points from your family members doesn't really make much sense."

(long pause)

Danger Monkey: "Minus ten points for Dad."

--- ■ ■ ■ ---

(in the car, kids yelling)

Me: "Kids! Too much! That's enough. No more yelling in the car. Never yell in the car."

Little Miss Thing, age seven: "No yelling ... EVER?"

Me: "The only thing you're allowed to yell is, 'DAD IS COOL.'"

Danger Monkey, age ten: "In other words, no yelling EVER."

--- ■ ■ ■ ---

Danger Monkey, age ten: "Your beef stew is delicious, but it has too many vegetables."

Me: "Vegetables are part of the soup. It's yummy. Eat up."

Danger Monkey: "This should be called 'Vegetable Soup with a Tiny Bit of Beef.'"

Me: "Actually, wiseguy, it's got plenty of ..."

Danger Monkey: "I'm going to make Beef Stew that's just one kernel of corn and the rest is beef and delicious broth."

(long pause)

Me: "As your father I'm supposed to correct you, but I would totally eat that."

--- ▪ ▪ ▪ ---

(boy climbs into the car)

Me: "We're just going into town to pick up some things. Why did you run back into the house?"

Danger Monkey, age ten: "I almost forgot my dice. I have a special pocket in my fleece just for my dice bag and some pencils in case anyone ever wants to play D&D."

Me: (sniff)

Danger Monkey: "Daddy, are you crying?"

--- ▪ ▪ ▪ ---

Danger Monkey, age four: "When I'm a grown-up, I won't work. I'll just stay home and play with my kids."

Me: "Really? If you don't have a job, where will you get food?"

(long pause)

Danger Monkey: "The kitchen."

Guy Talk

My son crawled under his big, fluffy comforter, flopping onto his back. I leaned over and gave him a long, snuggly hug, then stood up.

"Good night, my boy. Get some good sleep. I love you. You're smart and strong and kind and funny and hard working. I'm proud to be your dad," I said, turning to leave.

He pulled the big blanket up to his chin. "Yeah, but you're my dad. You have to say that."

I stopped and turned back to him. "No, actually, I don't," I replied. "In fact, many dads never say those things. I think most of them think it but don't feel comfortable saying it out loud. So they say it in other ways."

His brow furled. "Why don't they say it?"

"Well, the truth of the world is that people are weird about how a man should act," I said, trying to not sound too judgmental. "A long time ago, boys were taught to not show their emotions at all. They were told that especially showing sadness or crying would make them seem weak." I shrugged my shoulders. "Even when I was little, I was taught that boys shouldn't cry."

He rolled toward me with confusion on his face. "But Mom says crying is good for you."

"It is good for you," I said confidently. "No, I very much disagree with the idea that boys can't cry." I scooted him over a bit and sat on the bed next to him. "I think showing emotion makes us stronger and happier in every way. In fact, I'm trying very hard to raise you without restrictions on showing your emotions or how you get to feel or not feel."

I tousled his hair a bit. "But I'm sure in sixth grade you're already getting a different story from friends at school."

He sat quiet in thought, clearly recalling conversations with school friends. "Sometimes, I guess."

"It's a hard line to draw. Men are expected to be strong, but actually we have to let out our emotions, too," I said. "And that's exactly why I talk about my emotions with you. I want to show you that big, strong men absolutely talk about our feelings. We can be sad and mushy and proud and whatever we want."

"That does seem better," he said, contemplating my words.

"Yeah, it's not always that simple, but I think it's a good place to start."

We sat for a while without speaking, just listening to the night sounds in his darkened room. Eventually, he quietly asked, "So other dads don't say those things?"

"I think most don't say them out loud. Neither my dad nor my step-dad ever said those things to me when I was growing up. I think most dads don't actually say the words as much as they probably should."

"Huh," he said with a tone of surprise.

"Don't get me wrong. Dads all show their love in other ways, like making up silly nicknames and rough housing in the living room."

His face lit up with recognition. "Is that why you make up so many names for us?"

"Yes, Rufus," I chuckled. "That's exactly why I call you so many different names."

He broke into a mischievous smile. "Why did you call me Rufus, you Big Butt Face?"

"Gosh, I don't know, Smack Daniels, why do you think?"

He giggled. "Because you love me, Poop Face."

I giggled, too. "You got it, Barf Boy."

He launched a surprise attack, lunging at me to wrestle. We lock arms and tussled a bit before I broke away. "OK, OK," I said with my dad voice. "No more wrestling. It's time to wind down for sleeping, not to get all worked up."

He settled back and pulled the cover back up protectively, still flush with the thrill of battle.

I patted his head gently. "You know, kiddo, most dads are more comfortable showing their love by working hard at their jobs to provide for their families and by being strong and protecting their kids." I tucked his blanket under his chin. "Those are ways that almost everyone agrees that dads should show their love."

"Those are good ways," he said.

"They sure are. Also, remember that most dads are more athletic than I am, so they do sports things with their sons, like taking them running or coaching their soccer teams. That's their way of showing their love. I buy groceries and cook food for you guys. That's more my way of showing my love."

"And you teach us how to cook," he said brightly.

"Absolutely," I said. "That is definitely one of the ways I show my love."

He sat quietly for a bit, pondering. "But other dads don't say the words?"

"They think it," I said. "But it's hard to say it sometimes."

"So why do you say all that stuff?"

"Because kids need to hear those things," I said. "Really, everyone needs to hear those things, but especially kids. Too much of your life will be the whole world telling you what's wrong with you. I want you to start life with a nice solid foundation of knowing what is RIGHT with you. Doesn't that sound better?"

His brow was still furled as he carefully chose his answer. "I like it, but only if you really mean it."

"Yes," I replied. "I really, really do. I mean it more than you will understand until you have your own kids."

I stood up from his bed and faced him. The room was still and peaceful as moonlight played across his comforter. The ceiling fan purred quietly above us, humming its long, simple song.

"Good night. I love you, Garbage Face," he said softly.

"I love you, too, beautiful boy. Get some good sleep."

Some Like It Hot

You don't get to choose what you remember
about your dad. Mine wasn't around a lot, and
when he was — well, he wasn't what you'd call a
role model. So I never really learned to use tools,
or tie a Windsor knot, or talk sports like all the
other guys. But life is not all sports and tools. I
like to focus on the good things he gave me, like
my sense of humor, a joy of learning and
especially his amazing ability to see the wonder in
everything, big and small.

My favorite memory of my dad is kind of dumb,
really. I visited him only once in California, and
one day he took me with him on a job. I rode in

the van, and climbed the ladder up onto the roof, and handed him tools. That's a big deal to an eight-year-old boy.

I remember helping him feed a giant coiled-wire brush down into an exhaust pipe. It was a sunny day in Southern California, also known as the Mojave Desert. I remember the roof being extremely hot and we were both sweating. We drank lots of water and he gave me a salt pill. He said, "It's good to take salt pills when you're working out in the sun." It was so cool. I still think salt pills are magical.

Lunch was Mexican. Living so near the border, he scoffed at the watered down, Americanized places. "Only real, authentic Mexican food for hard workingmen like us," he said. For the life of me, I couldn't tell you what we ordered. I just remember his eyes watering and his brow dripping with sweat, even more than when we were in the sun. "The sauce," he said. "It's super hot, but so good. You can't get this kind of flavor without the heat." I was in awe. He was my idol.

To this day, I love eating all the hottest foods I can find.

I spent my 30s really angry at my dad for a lot of reasons, but mostly because he died. Just like when I was three years old, he had left us again. He died just as I started to have my own kids, right as I started to understand how hard it is and see how it's not just cuddles and diapers and bad drawings on your fridge. He left before I could tell him that I finally understood how it pulls you down a little every day, how the weight of it can feel like it's crushing your soul. I finally saw for myself how easy it would be to run away to California.

You can't truly forgive someone until you know their struggle.

But for me, by the time I knew what to say, it was too late. Dad took his own life after decades of battling addictions and depression. It happened just weeks after we shared tears of joy when I handed him my first child, still shiny and wee. I can still see him looking at her with such intense affection, as if his heart would burst. She cooed at him, like a four-month-old baby does, and then rewarded him with diarrhea on his shirt. He whipped off his shirt without a word and held her to his chest, skin on skin. His smile never dimmed. It's a wonderful memory that I will always treasure. It's hard to believe it was our last time together.

Maybe that's the price we pay for perspective and wisdom. Maybe it's like hot sauce — you can't get to the good stuff without the heat. Maybe it takes loss and pain to unlock the parts of us that need to be unlocked. Maybe his absence and inconsistency are what gave me my strength and persistence. Maybe I'm a better person because of his failures. Maybe it's easier to tell myself that. Maybe I'm just grasping.

Regardless, now I'm the dad and I freely admit I'm not great at it. Sure, I try to pass on my humor and love of learning and a sense of wonder, just like my dad did. I'm also trying to teach my kids about tools and tying ties and sports, but it's hard. Mostly, I'm showing up and hanging around and just being there.

Somewhere along the way I figured out that being a dad is not tools or ties or money or wisdom. It's not what you say, it's where you say it. It's just being there for them.

So, here I am.

My kids love to hear stories about my dad. They howl at all the pranks he pulled and jokes he told and all the crazy amazing stuff he did. They love all the good parts, and they know him as the loving father he wanted to be. They'll never know him like I did, not his pain or his anger or failures. But I want them to know his good side, to know his virtues. I feel I owe that to him, and I owe it to them. Mostly, I owe that to myself.

Lately my car tends to steer us toward authentic Mexican restaurants. Just last week my nine-year-old son tried some of my hot sauce and was surprised that I could eat something so spicy. "It's super hot, but so good," I told him. "You can't get this kind of flavor without the heat."

He looked at me with awe in his eyes. "I want to eat really spicy food, too," he said.

"I know, son. I know you do."

Let's just say it's a good thing my eyes were already watering.

My Oldest

(we see girls wearing ripped jeans)

Me: "Ooh, are ripped jeans in again?"

My Oldest, age twelve: "Yes, they're very popular."

Me: "Cool! I'd love to start wearing all my old ripped jeans again."

(pause)

My Oldest: "No, I was wrong … Ripped jeans are *not* in. Let's pretend I never said that."

--- ■ ■ ■ ---

My Oldest, age twelve: "The Hindenburg. Wasn't that where everyone was like, 'Hey, this is a great idea!' And then BOOM, and everyone was like, 'Wow, that was a horrible idea'?"

Me: "Yep, you pretty much nailed it."

--- ■ ■ ■ ---

Me: "I think I'll start posting lots of selfies on Facebook. Selfies are healthy for your self-image."

My Oldest, age thirteen: "Then I need $6,000."

Me: "What? Why is that?"

My Oldest: "That's how much it costs to change my identity."

--- ■ ■ ■ ---

My Oldest, age thirteen: "No offense, but I'll never bring dates to this house. They'll take one look at Daddy and say, 'It's not you — it's me.' And run away."

--- ■ ■ ■ ---

My Oldest, age thirteen: "I accidentally put the dog's pajamas on her backwards. For the record, it's really hard to take off dog pajamas while the dog is trying to kill you."

Me: "I'm on the dog's side on this one."

My Oldest: "You never support my hobbies."

--- ■ ■ ■ ■ ---

Me: "I love you."

My Oldest, age fourteen: "How much?"

Me: "Should you be murdered, I will avenge your death in a blind rage."

My Oldest: "That's solid ... But don't get caught. And try to invent a poison that makes them cough up glitter as they die."

Me: "As you wish."

--- ■ ■ ■ ■ ---

Me: "Hey, do you know that young couple over there?"

My Oldest, age fourteen: "Yes. They go to my school. Why do you ask?"

Me: "They keep looking over here and are about your age, so I figured maybe they were trying to get your attention or something."

My Oldest: "Or maybe they just aren't good at not getting caught staring at giant, hairy Hagrid-looking dudes."

Me: "Noted."

--- ■ ■ ■ ---

Me: "Are you still dating that one ..."

My Oldest, age fourteen: "Yes."

Me: "Good. I approve."

My Oldest: "I don't need your approval."

Me: "No, but it's nice for your parents to approve of your significant others. It says a lot about your choices."

(long pause)

My Oldest: "Actually, I think I'm the one the other parents worry about."

Me: "Nice."

(fist bump)

--- ■ ■ ■ ---

My Oldest, age fourteen: "Some of these snarky internet videos are actually informational."

Me: "Yeah, right. Ha. Ha. Very funny."

My Oldest: "No, really. Like 'The History of Japan.' It's hilarious and rude, and now I know how the U.S. forces invaded Japan under Matthew Perry, and …"

Me: "MATTHEW Perry? Hahahahaha! Chandler Bing invaded Japan? Hahahahaha!"

My Oldest: "What?"

Me: "I think you meant COMMODORE Perry."

My Oldest: "Yes, Commodore Matthew Perry."

Me: "Wait ... his first name was Matthew?"

My Oldest: "Maybe you should watch more internet videos."

--- ■ ■ ■ ■ ---

Danger Monkey, age nine: "Hey! I didn't say 'GO' yet!"

My Oldest, age fifteen: "Life has no start or stop buttons. I'm preparing you for real life. You're welcome."

Danger Monkey: "Well, I don't like it."

My Oldest: "No one does."

Me: "You are bitter beyond your years."

My Oldest: "Thank you."

--- ■ ■ ■ ■ ---

Me: "Let's try a different restaurant tonight."

My Oldest, age fifteen: "Nope."

Me: "Awww, why not? We can't always go to the same three restaurants."

My Oldest: "Uh. Yes, we can."

Me: "Where's your spirit of adventure?"

My Oldest: "There's a reason we go to the same ones — they're good. If you want to try Uncle Stinky's Barbecue & Foot Spa, or whatever, then do it on your own time."

Me: "Wait, is that place real? It sounds awesome."

My Oldest: "Aaaaand, there's your problem."

--- ■ ■ ■ ---

My Oldest, age fifteen: "Can I drive home? I have my permit now."

Me: "Sure."

My Oldest: (starts engine) "Bwahaha! I'm the driver now! We're going to Dairy Queen and there's nothing you can do about it! I'm in control! You have to go where I want to go!"

(long pause)

My Oldest: "You're still going to pay, right?"

--- ■ ■ ■ ---

My Oldest, age sixteen: "Wow, I love all the new framed art you have in the house."

Me: "Yeah, about that."

My Oldest: "What about it?"

Me: "I won them all in an auction. The good news is the money went to a very good cause."

My Oldest: "And the bad news?"

Me: "We can't pay for your college. Sorry, honey."

My Oldest: "That's OK. Now I'll just have to win some scholarship and when they hand me the giant cardboard check people will look at the picture and say, 'Why isn't she smiling?' and someone will say, 'Oh, it looks like she's glaring at someone just off camera'."

--- ■ ■ ■ ---

My Oldest, age sixteen: "What is all that noise upstairs? Those kids were tucked in an hour ago. How can you not hear all that stomping? Are they having a dance party? Please tell me you can hear that."

Me: "If I hear it, then I have to do something about it. Do you want to do something about it?"

(long pause)

My Oldest: "You're right. I can't hear a thing."

--- ■ ■ ■ ---

My Oldest, age sixteen, eating potato chips: "Since when do you hide potato chips from us?"

Me: "SHHHHH!"

Me: (whispering) "I don't hide them. I just store them ... strategically. And please be quiet before the others hear you."

My Oldest: "This from the guy who taught us to not keep secrets. Nice."

Me: "Hey, now, cut me a little slack. I only hide them because you kids snarf them up immediately as soon as you know they're in the house. It's one of my only treats, so I like them to last longer than ten minutes."

My Oldest: "Whatever. I guess you can hide all the barbecue chips you want, I just want the plain ones."

Danger Monkey, age ten: (from the other room) "We have barbecue chips! Woo-hoo!"

Me: (glaring)

My Oldest, batting eye lashes: "Love you, Daddy."

(walks away)

There Will Be a Test

Her backpack thudded to a stop on the bench as she slid gracefully into our regular booth. "Why do we keep coming to this Chinese buffet? There are, like, five Thai restaurants nearby."

I lacked her grace as I wedged my bulk into the opposite bench. "Oh, I know that. But this is the only place where I can make sure we both get some veggies. Also, they don't care if you spread out your homework and study for a couple hours."

"Yeah. That's probably why I don't like it," she said, pulling a heavy textbook out of her bag.

"Hey, let's change it up and eat first this week. I have a theory that humans digest our food better when we separate eating from working." I gestured her toward the buffet. "There's plenty of time to study later. I'll watch your books. Go get some food."

She paused as if to make a snarky comment but changed her mind and stood.

"And I'm serious, don't forget the veggies."

Her eyes rolled as she left, but she returned with green beans alongside the usual starches.

"Hey, look, green veggies! You may live to see age sixteen after all."

"Oh, ha ha. I get green beans every time. And why the concern? I eat better than you do."

"Well, that's your opinion. You eat less than I do, sure. But these days I'm eating more protein and veggies. Mostly just less processed crap," I said, scooting out of the booth. "I worry that you're not getting enough vitamins sometimes."

"I eat what I like. You always say we should listen to our bodies, and this is what my body wants." She twirled a noodle around her fork, slurping it noisily into her mouth. "Mmmmm ... carbs."

"Don't talk with your mouth full," I said, not hiding my smile as I left her there, chewing loudly for my benefit.

I returned soon enough with a crowded plate of all my favorites, and we ate together. Between bites, I talked about my work and told her stories about her younger siblings' hi-jinx from the week. She shared energetic stories about her friends, her thoughts on gender politics and which bands were playing nearby.

Eventually she pushed her plate away and reached for her textbooks. "I have so much studying to do," she mumbled with the heavy sigh of the downtrodden.

"You really do study a lot. But that's pretty much your job at this point in life," I said, taking a big bite of chicken from a stick. "Whereas my job is finding more meats served on sticks," I said, chewing loudly.

"Don't talk with your mouth full," she said with a sly grin.

"You got me." I swallowed and showed her my empty mouth, sticking out my tongue.

"Ewwww. Gross! You're gross."

I chuckled. "You know you're good at what you do, right?"

"At busting you for breaking your own rules? Yeah, I'm great at it."

"No, I mean that you're a great student, a great kid. I'm sure it doesn't feel like it because you're in the middle of it, and you're still growing. But — you're nailing it."

She stared at me, eyebrow raised, trying to read any hint of sarcasm on my face.

"No, I mean it, kiddo. From my heart. You're learning to study more efficiently every week. You're keeping up your grades, all the while having fun side activities, too." I scooped up a piece of General Tso's Chicken. "I mean, you're fifteen. It's important to have fun."

"Oh. My. God. I work so hard! All of my classes are either honors or AP. It's impossible to do all the homework they assign us. Plus, orchestra and Girl Scouts and 4-H and babysitting. Also, keep in mind I'm in a band, which is fun, but still a lot of work." Her eyebrows scrunched. "It's amazing that I get any sleep at all."

"I love that you're so musically talented and I'm amazed you still have the energy to be in a band. You're a pretty cool kid."

"Kid!? I'm a young woman, thank you very much." She smirked, but her stare didn't waver. "Wait. Are you trying to butter me up or something?"

"Maybe," I shrugged. "Or, maybe, just maybe, I'm really proud of my daughter and I think she deserves to hear it. In fact," I said, pointing my fork for emphasis. "I think you should hear it as often as possible."

Her eyes turned back to her homework. "Yeah, whatever."

I chased a wonton around my plate for a minute, then gave up. "So, what are we studying this week? World history again?"

"Physics. We have a test on Friday and I'm a little stuck."

"Oh, physics! I love physics. And don't sweat the test. There will always be a test."

"That's not helping. Can you look at number 27? They give us all these factors, but I can't figure out where the vectors are." She tapped her pencil in frustration.

"Ah, yes. Vectors are fun. Lemme see."

She spun the paper around so I could see it. "Vector's aren't fun. They're irritating."

"Thank you, I will accept 'gross' as a compliment," I said, examining the page. "We all enjoy what we enjoy. I really enjoy math and science. They're just sets of logical rules to help explain what's happening around us."

She sat up and leaned toward the paper. "Yeah, I like math. I love physics. It's just that the class is so stressful with all my other stuff going on."

"Oh, I'm sure. Maybe you need to spend more time on it. But that's for another discussion. I see your problem here," I said as I turned the paper back to her. "You have to remember that the point of defining vectors is to show the two forces that are being exerted on a single object from two different angles. But an object can't go two different directions. The object goes in one direction, and that resulting direction is influenced by both vectors, according to each vector's strength."

Her eyes narrowed a bit. "Yeah, OK — I think I get that. So the answer — the answer is what the object does, because the two vectors moved it." She started writing rapidly across the paper. "Yeah, OK. So you basically just draw a rectangle

— using the two vectors as sides for your rectangle — and the result is the diagonal across the rectangle. OK."

"Yeah, see, you've got it." I leaned back.

Her hand moved smoothly back and forth, sketching and computing. "OK. I get this now."

I chuckled. "I'm glad I can help a little. I still enjoy that stuff. I guess it helps that you're my rectangle."

Her hand stopped and she looked up. "I'm your what?"

"You are my rectangle. I'm just one of the vectors that influences your life. All of us: your mother, your step-mother, your friends, your teachers. We influence you, but you make your own trajectory."

She sighed loudly. "Mm-hmm. Here you go again."

I reached across the cluttered table and touched her hand. "No, I'm serious. Your life has all these influences. You're getting it from all sides. I get it. I was in your shoes not that long ago."

"It was pretty long ago."

"Very funny. And yes, technology has changed but high school hasn't. I know that you've got people giving you shit every day and you're just trying to do the best you can. I know that we ask too much of you, but I also know that you're up to the challenge."

She looked away. "I don't always feel up to the challenge."

"Of course not. But you are. You really are," I said, leaning forward again. "Believe it or not, I know exactly what it's like to crave independence so badly you can taste it. You want to fly, but you also know you still need a safety net. It's incredibly frustrating."

She looked back at me. "So frustrating."

I looked into her eyes. "You are doing something truly remarkable, kiddo. You are creating a new person, a new personality, from scratch. And it's ridiculously hard work. You're making difficult decisions every minute of every day. You're cobbling together bits and pieces of all these sources, all these influences. You've got a million vectors moving you, and you get to choose which vectors influence you more than others. Those choices help to create who you become. The final trajectory is all you."

She held my gaze. "That almost made sense. You are so sappy."

"Hey, all I ask is that you let me continue to be in your equation. I just want my vector to be part of the push on your object. Or on you. Or something. I lost the metaphor."

"You've lost more than that."

"Hush. Now, the big complication is I'm your Dad and protecting you is part of every fiber of my being. It's not a decision I make as much as just who I am. So, I'm obligated to tell you to always, always question those other influences. Yes, some of them are cooler than me, and all suave and hip and up on all the cool slang. But they don't usually have your best interest in mind."

She rolled her eyes. "Yeah, OK, Dad. Whatever."

"Hey, c'mon now, hear me out."

"Yeah, yeah. Don't freak out. I'm listening."

"This is important. I need you to know in your heart as you go through your day that I always have your best interest in mind, no matter how lame it comes across when I show it." I squeezed her hand gently. "I always have been and always will be trying to help you become the best person you can be. Whatever that means for you." I retracted my hand from her side of the table and slouched back into my seat. "Whether you like it or not."

She looked down and started working on the problem again. "I know all of that. I know you're looking out for me."

I took a last bite of my food, and this time swallowed before speaking. "I'm really proud of you, honey. You are the greatest achievement of my entire life," I said, setting down my fork. "And I just want my vector to be in that rectangle."

She chuckled and shook her head softly. "Whatever." She didn't look up from her work. "I love you, Dad."

"I know you do."

I pushed my plate away and let the moment quietly pass. I sat there and enjoyed the somber scratching of the pencil pushing her thoughts onto paper.

"So, tell me. Do you think your friends have dads that say all this gross stuff?"

She continued intently working her problem. As the pencil scratched the paper, I heard her quietly mumble, "Maybe. If they're lucky."

Fly Away

My best friend was in town recently. He's an amazing guy and has been with me through thick and thin. I'm not sure how I would have gotten through my divorce and all the challenges over the years without his unwavering support. He's been a constant in my life and a source of stability that I don't know how I could ever repay. So I treated him to my favorite Sunday brunch buffet, because that's about as sincere a thank you as I know of.

For over an hour we indulged in the glory of cooked-to-order omelets, roast beef au jus and bottomless bacon as we remembered stories about our younger days and how we met each other as college freshmen. I was the guy in our dorm that had some wild room parties during freshman orientation. He was the guy that wore a funny hat around campus and told bad jokes. It was a crazy time of new friends, intense learning, and drinking too much, too often. Those two young guys are just memories now, but it made for a lovely afternoon of reminiscing and laughing at old stories.

That afternoon, after we had eaten and laughed for a long time, he pushed his plate away and said, "I hope you're more prepared than I was."

"Oh, yeah?" I said. "I think I was prepared. I ate my fair share."

"No, not the buffet." He said.

"Then what?" I replied.

He got a far away look in his eyes. "It all goes by so fast, man. Just make sure you appreciate the time you have."

"You OK, dude?" I said, wiping a bit of sausage gravy off my shirt.

He swallowed hard. "I just wasn't prepared emotionally, man. I wasn't ready when it hit me," he said as he shook his head. "I mean — I can't believe I just dropped off my son to start college."

I gave him a sincere look, trying my best to impart all the warmth and empathy that can be expected from an emotionally stunted man-child like myself.

"You're a good dad," I told him. "I'm sure your son is having the time of his life."

"Yeah," he said. "That's what I'm afraid of."

"Oh, he'll be fine," I said reassuringly. And then I politely changed the subject back to food, because real men aren't allowed to discuss their feelings for more than thirty seconds.

But I think I know those feelings. I grumbled for years about all the driving I was doing taking My Oldest back and forth between her mother's house and my own. Even with her mother's taking half the driving, it was a lot of miles. But suddenly My Oldest is sixteen and she just got her driver's license. She's mobile and free. She doesn't need the old man for transportation.

I do a lot less driving now, but what shocked me is that I miss it. I miss it a lot. Gone are the many hours of talking one-on-one with her, hearing her thoughts, watching her slowly grow into a really cool young woman. As I stood and proudly watched her carefully drive off that day, my eyes welled with tears. It all hit me, and I suddenly wished I could have it all back. These days I have a hole in my heart that echoes with all my complaints about driving her.

So, why all the feelings? We've known all along that we are raising our kids to be strong and independent, to live their own lives. That's the goal, isn't it? Launching a responsible, successful adult child into the world is the Gold Medal of parenting. They have to live their lives, make their mistakes. Robbing them of that experience would be a crime.

The reality is that Real Life is scary. So much crime and accidents and terrorism and threats of nuclear war are all over the news. It's so hard to not be over-protective. I feel their pain so vividly, so completely. Every scrape, every needle prick, every broken heart — I would take their pain for them without hesitation. The urge is so strong to build walls around them and keep them safely under my wing. But I can't and I shouldn't and I won't. They have to make their own way.

I remember the exhilaration and freedom of getting my license. My first car was a '69 Camaro. And not just a muscle car with virtually no safety features, but literally a retired drag racer that had been tweaked and over-bored into a hulking, squealing, throaty monster. The seat belts were obligatory, perfunctory at best. There was nothing even resembling safety, and the term "airbag" meant something totally different in 1987. There was as much rust as there was metal. The brakes were shot, the exhaust system defunct. Over the life of that car, it never did have a dashboard. Yet

I loved that ugly, smelly, dangerous beast like nothing I had ever loved before.

Let's be clear — it was not a safe car, and I was not a safe driver. No sixteen-year-old boy should have ever been given that rally-striped death trap with 350 cubic inches under the hood. I smoked the tires at stop lights. I did donuts in the school parking lot until thick black circles were visible from space. I roared down every highway and byway, oblivious to speed limits or my mortality. And, late one night, I found out that the laws of physics and sharp turns on gravel roads don't care if you're on a date with your biggest crush. In the end, $F = ma$ whether you like it or not, Romeo.

But I lived through it all. I'm not really sure *how* I survived it, but I did. And, truth be told, I'm a fairly safe driver now. A little aggressive, but also very defensive. And she's a fairly safe driver, too. Much of what we talked about on all those drives together was how to drive defensively, how to predict what other drivers are doing, how to stay away from trouble. I also taught her that it's always OK to go a little slower, to not feel pressure to go fast. Unlike myself at sixteen, she's actually a fantastic, safe driver.

Most importantly, she's not driving a death trap. She's got our old Honda minivan and is thrilled with it. She likes that it can fit all her band's gear for gigs, and we love that it's one of the safest vehicles on the road. It's not pretty, with dings and scrapes and a couple of body parts literally held on with duct tape. But it's dependable and fuel efficient and it's her freedom. She loves it.

And, for the record, I also bought her some skull and crossbones decals, because life is not just about safety.

So, I guess that's my answer. Being a parent means preparing them the best you can, then ultimately trusting them to fly on their own. You have to allow them to make and learn from their own mistakes. But that doesn't mean you can't anticipate and try to pad their falls a bit. Who knew that anti-lock brakes and side-impact airbags were such a sincere way to show my love?

As my friend and I walked out of the restaurant that day, he chuckled and said, "Do you suppose my son will do all the crazy stuff we did in college?"

I looked him in the eye and said, "Yeah, probably. And he'll do all the good stuff we did, too. And probably more. In fact, he might just meet his best friend today."

"That would be cool," he said.

"Yeah," I replied. "It really would."

How to Raise Viking Children

Parenting is standing at the front door during a night storm, with a tiny, scared girl on your hip, calmly teaching her to count the gap between the lightning and the thunder, just like your dad taught you a million years ago. The hardest part is pretending you're not a little afraid of the lightning yourself.

--- ■ ■ ■ ---

Wonderful Wife: "We're going to have a sitter come over and watch you kids on Saturday."

Little Miss Thing, age five: "But why?"

Wonderful Wife: "So Daddy and I can go on a date."

Little Miss Thing: "Why?"

Wonderful Wife: "So we can spend time together and see a movie."

Little Miss Thing: "WHY?"

Wonderful Wife: "Because we love each other and like spending time together."

Little Miss Thing: "… Without US?"

--- ■ ■ ■ ---

Little Miss Thing, age seven: "Daddy, why do you have white hairs in your beard?"

Danger Monkey, age ten: "He has them in his hair, too. See … there and there and there. They're all over."

Little Miss Thing: "They're kind of silver. How did they get there?"

Me: "They're called grey hairs. It just happens naturally as we get older. Almost everyone over forty has some grey hair."

Danger Monkey: "Really?"

Me: "Yes, really."

Danger Monkey: "So ... I'll get grey hair when I'm old?"

Me: "Yup. It's totally natural and nothing to be ashamed of. In fact, I kind of like my grey hair."

Little Miss Thing: "Everybody?"

Me: "Yup."

Little Miss Thing: "Wait a minute ... Mom doesn't have any grey hair."

(long pause)

Me: "Nope, she sure doesn't."

--- ■ ■ ■ ---

Little Miss Thing, age six: "Can you help me find a hammer?"

Me: "Sure, honey. Where did you last see it?"

Little Miss Thing: "In the back yard."

Me: "Can you be more specific?"

Little Miss Thing: "Behind the woodpile."

Me: "Behind the woodpile is just a giant mess of thorns and seven-foot-tall weeds. How did a hammer get back there?"

Little Miss Thing: "I threw it."

Me: "And you want me to help you find it. After you threw it. Into the weeds."

Little Miss Thing: "Yes."

Me: "What does the hammer look like?"

Little Miss Thing: "It's green."

Me: "Of course it is."

--- ■ ■ ■ ---

Little Miss Thing, age six: "Dad, what is Campus Torturing Center?"

Me: "No, honey, not *TORTURING* Center. That's the Campus *TUTORING* Center."

(pause)

Little Miss Thing: "What's the difference?"

(long pause)

Me: "You know ... I can't think of any."

--- ■ ■ ■ ■ ---

Wonderful Wife: "Please use your fork, not fingers. We don't eat spaghetti with our hands."

Little Miss Thing, age seven: "Uh ... Nope."

Wife: "That wasn't a question. Try, 'Yes, Mama.'"

Little Miss Thing: "Nope. I don't feel like it."

Me: (clears throat) "That was strike two, kiddo. If you don't respond appropriately to your mother, immediately, there will be serious consequences."

Little Miss Thing: "Like what?"

Me: "Like ... losing all your electronics for a day."

Little Miss Thing: "I don't care."

Me: "OK, wise guy. How about for a week?"

Little Miss Thing: "I don't care."

Me: "Hmmm. Then I guess I'll have to take away that new stuffed animal you bought last ..."

Little Miss Thing: "Sorry, Mama. I won't do it again."

--- ■ ■ ■ ■ ---

What my kids learned today:

1) Sometimes a blinking red light on the dash means the engine is almost totally out of oil.

2) When stopping at a gas station to buy oil, always ask the cashier for a free paper funnel.

3) When carrying several oil bottles and a free paper funnel on a windy day, hold on tightly.

4) When the free paper funnel goes blowing across the parking lot and into the street, always

send your son back inside to get another one so you don't have to admit you lost the first one.

5) After removing the engine oil cap, set it in a safe place. *NEVER* place it on the engine block.

6) When the oil cap slides off the engine block and down into the guts of the engine compartment, Daddy will say bad words.

7) It is very hard to dislodge an oil cap from the guts of an engine compartment, even with a very large Viking jumping up and down on the front bumper.

8) The residents of small Midwestern towns are not accustomed to seeing very large Vikings jumping up and down on bumpers.

9) In emergencies, you can jam a wad of paper towel into the hole and drive three blocks to an auto parts store.

10) A replacement oil cap costs $8.89, plus tax, and a heaping helping of your pride.

--- ■ ■ ■ ■ ---

Wonderful Wife: "The boy is going to his first school dance tonight."

Me: "Whoa! What? Should I have a talk with him? Yes, I need to talk to him. What if a girl asks him to dance? Does he know how to slow dance? Or fast dance? He's growing up so fast. I'm not ready for him to have his first kiss or anything. This is too soon. So much we need to talk about."

(deep breath)

Me: "Hey, son ..."

(boy runs up)

Me: "So, my boy. Are you excited about the dance?"

Danger Monkey, age nine: "No. I'm hoping me and the guys can have a pickup soccer game or something. Why? Did you want to talk about something?"

Me: "Nah, we're good. Have fun tonight."

--- ■ ■ ■ ■ ---

Wonderful Wife: "Family, we will be getting up tomorrow at 7 o'clock."

Little Miss Thing, age six: "Awwww."

Wonderful Wife: "Oh, I suppose you would prefer 8 o'clock?"

Little Miss Thing: "How about ... EIGHTY o'clock?"

Wonderful Wife: "She gets that from you."

Me: "What? Sorry. I was daydreaming about getting to sleep until eighty o'clock."

--- ▪ ▪ ▪ ---

Me: "Kids, this is called Flan. It's a type of custard that's covered in liqueur, so it's illegal for kids to eat it."

My Oldest, age fifteen: "Sounds gross."

Danger Monkey, age eight: "I will never eat that until I'm at least 21 years old."

Little Miss Thing, age five: "I want it."

--- ▪ ▪ ▪ ---

Me: "Hey! Who left the back door totally open? The air conditioning costs money, you know!"

Danger Monkey, age ten: "Sorry. I forgot to close it."

Me: "Please try harder to remember in the future. It really does cost money."

Danger Monkey: "OK. Sorry. I'll go close it."

Me: "No, I'll close it for you. It's starting to rain, so I'll just go out and put the cover on my grill real quick."

Little Miss Thing, age seven: "In your UNDERWEAR?"

Me: "Sure, why not?"

Little Miss Thing: "You can't go outside in your underwear!"

Me: "We live out in the woods and no one can see our back deck. And what's the difference between boxer shorts and swimming trunks?"

Little Miss Thing: "I think it's a really bad idea."

Danger Monkey: "Yeah, Dad. I really think you don't want to go out there."

Me: "Well, guess what? Just to clear things up around here, I'm the adult and I've been around the block a time or two. So I think I can make this type of decision for myself. Trust me, it's not as big a deal as you think. But thanks for your input and your concern."

Me: (steps outside)

(door slams behind me)

(door locks loudly)

Me: "Uh …"

(laughter behind the door)

(so much laughter)

(mass hysterics)

(rain starts to fall)

Me: "I really should have seen that coming."

--- ■ ■ ■ ---

(at school picnic)

Wonderful Wife: "It's been about half an hour since they checked in. Can you see our kids?"

Me: "Lemme look."

(stands up, scans large field of active children)

Wonderful Wife: "And?"

Me: "Yes, I can see them. They're good."

Wonderful Wife: "What are they doing?"

Me: "He's with a group of his friends and it looks like they're daring each other to eat dirt. She's chasing some older boys and throwing sticks at them."

(long pause)

Wonderful Wife: "Sounds about right."

Me: "Situation Normal."

(sits back down)

--- ■ ■ ■ ■ ---

<u>Things I Have Actually, Literally Said</u>:

"No, just because you can fit half an avocado into your mouth does not make it 'bite-sized'."

"Come down right now and get your giant squid."

"Your argument is persuasive, but in most states a bad mood does not justify physical assault."

"My pancreas is not a trampoline."

"It is sad that you can't be a dog when you grow up, but veterinarian is close."

"Please stop demonstrating lemur fighting techniques at the dinner table."

"Is that music coming from your room, or is someone trapped and signaling for help?"

"Let's try for less death stares at your little sister at the dinner table, please."

"No, you may not wear just a cape and a clip-on tie to bed."

"You must stop pretending to barf on your sisters."

"We do not use bungee cords as weapons."

"No kick-fighting in the car, please."

"Yes, this is a long trip, but you are five years old. You do not get a turn driving."

"Look, kids. This is not negotiable. We are a fresh-underwear-every-day kind of family."

"You absolutely may not use the word 'poop' when writing someone a birthday card."

"No, licking off the icing and throwing away the cupcake is not considered 'Low Carb'."

"It's pronounced 'BYOOT'. There is no such place as 'BUTT' Montana."

"Last time I checked, the ABC song did not include the word 'poop'."

"Kids, this is a school carnival, so I guess you can keep the balloons in your shirt, but you must stop yelling, 'I'VE GOT BOOBS'."

What I Missed

Back in the day, we never seemed to have enough clothes to wear or food to eat, let alone fancy video games or the latest toy. So we kids played outside all the time. It wasn't a decision — that's just what you do when you're broke. But, if I recall correctly, trees, dirt, and a complete lack of common sense are all free and can make for a solid afternoon.

In fact, I don't remember ever being bored as a child. I do remember running a lot, and falling down, and getting back up again. I drank from the hose and got that special kind of kid-dirty that adults can't muster. There was so much dirt and digging and puddles and look-how-far-I-can-slide-in-the-mud. I remember getting hurt and learning to be brave about it. One time I learned why maybe it isn't a great idea to play with matches on a dry, windy day.

I also remember the frequent flush of envy when other kids went out to dinner or to the movies or whatever it was they were doing without me. I remember hating that I was always playing at someone else's house. But they had that new robot that talked or a super-cool train set mounted on a board that folded out of the wall. I could have been grateful they shared with me, but, instead, it was a pinch and a gnawing in my gut that couldn't be reasoned with. Look, at a certain point, you notice that Santa gives the other kids more presents than he gives you. Which is a lot for a little kid to process.

I respect that I'm one of the lucky ones. I've worked hard and have had some successes in life, but a lot of people work hard and don't get the same opportunities. Poverty is not just a mindset or spending habits or laziness. It's an often inherited, insidious cycle that the majority never break. And even if you do break out, it's still part of you. It's baggage I still carry — and probably always will.

Fast forward a million years, and now I'm The Dad. My wife and I are educated, we stay busy, and we're doing all right. Of course, I buy too many video games and I make sure the kids have nice bikes. Last year, we even set up a somewhat pricey zip line out in the woods. Even I will admit that we probably eat out more than we should.

But, you see, I love to scoop them up in the evening and head into town. Dinner, yes please. Maybe a movie? They love that one ice cream stand, of course. It doesn't even matter to me where, or when, or why. It just makes me happy deep down that my kids get to have the things I wanted so badly as a kid.

However, as The Universe is so fond of reminding me, I'm not actually in charge. Tonight, the kids got home and hit the front door at sonic speed, dropped off their things, and immediately ran into the woods. No hello, no goodbye. Barely looked at me. The cats didn't even have time to ignore them properly. I can hear their shrill chorus along with all the neighbor kids screaming somewhere off in the trees. Don't they know I had big plans? Don't they care that I want to give them the things I didn't have? How ungrateful.

Like it or not, being an adult means you eventually realize some hard truths. Tonight my kids showed me that all my years of hurting and feeling left out were a giant waste of energy. What was I angry about, exactly? That I had to play outside? In the woods? With my friends? C'mon, dude — that's the good stuff.

These days, I'm seeing that new, shiny bikes don't matter, that the talking robot just ended up in a landfill. In the end, I don't regret not having fancy toys like a wall-mounted train set. My regret is that I spent so much of my childhood focused on what I didn't have that I never appreciated just how much I did have.

Tonight, we're not jet-setting in town like I had planned. We're staying home and eating leftovers, yet again. Sigh. Not because we can't afford it, but because my kids know what is important. They aren't hung up on price tags or ambient lighting or locally sourced organic saffron. They prefer romping and stomping and climbing and pretending to be a dog. Don't underestimate the importance of pretending to be a dog every once in a while.

The big thing is that my kids already appreciate what they have. So, I guess they are having the childhood I wanted after all. Huh. What do you know about that?

It took me 46 years to realize that happiness is about skipping the expensive zip line and playing in the mud instead.

Hey, now the kids are climbing trees. I think I even heard one of them fall. Maybe someone will get their arm in a cast, and all of their friends can sign it tomorrow. What great memories. How lucky would that be?

That Little Voice

An 8 am teeth cleaning is not my idea of a great start to my day, but it was nice to have a clear mission for a change. Between my relaxed schedule of working from home and being off work so much lately, I am definitely out of the habit of getting dressed and leaving the house in the morning. Falling back into the old routine helped me feel like my life is getting back to normal. I was even on time to the dentist, which is rare.

I really like my dentist and all her staff. The office is delightful and cheery, but not frivolous. It's a calm refuge. Perhaps a little too relaxing. I'm trying to not wear my feelings on my sleeve, so when the dental hygienist asked how I was doing, it surprised me as much as her when I blurted out that my mother had died. It was awkward for both of us. I regretted burdening her, and it didn't make me feel any better. She tripped over herself to be extra nice to me the rest of the visit.

Sigh.

After the teeth cleaning, I did the obvious thing and got a giant spicy breakfast burrito. It's my happy place. Don't judge me.

Leaving the restaurant, a crisp, white envelope on the sidewalk caught my eye. I started to ignore it, but a little voice in my head told me to turn back and pick it up. It was thick, as in "important stuff in here" kind of thick. It also had that intentionally generic look that banks use, and I could see the recipient's name and address in the little cellophane window. I didn't recognize the name, and the envelope had been opened and then folded. This was not trash. This had been dropped accidentally and losing it was probably going to ruin someone's day.

Well, it's the year 2017 and I have a smart phone, so I looked up the address and drove the envelope to its owner. It was only a few miles away and somewhat on my way home. Well, sort of on my way. OK, it was totally out of my way. Sue me.

As I pulled up at this random stranger's house, it occurred to me I should at least look him up on Facebook first. Turns out we have a few friends in common, so I opted to ring the doorbell instead of just stuffing it into the mailbox.

After a few moments, he opened the door hesitantly. It's not a subtle experience to have a 6'4", 400-pound, wild-haired Viking on your porch. Everyone opens their doors hesitantly. It's a thing.

I handed him his envelope. He was surprised and grateful, of course. He shook my hand, thanked me, and said he hadn't realized he had dropped it.

He was amazed I had brought it all the way to his house. Then his wife appeared and said hello and that she was sorry about my mom.

Wait ... what?

Look, I'll be super honest, I'm in a weird place right now. Life is busy, and I'm a giant Viking with responsibilities. I'm a role model for several precocious children who pick up on any whiff of insincerity. I take pride in being strong physically and emotionally for them. But when your Mom dies, even giant Vikings get a pass.

It's one of the few, possibly only, situations where grown, hairy-faced men are universally allowed to cry. I don't agree with that system, but it's the truth.

I simply don't like to cry. I was raised that real men don't cry, so it makes me feel weak and less of a man when I do it. And this week I've been flailing around in that prickly grey area between what I want, what I need, what I believe in and what society has ingrained. It's not a fun place to be.

Needless to say, my emotional reserves are thin. Watching your mom slowly decline over a couple of years ... it stresses you in odd ways. Deep ways. Every trip to the emergency room, every event you cancel, every time you help her down the stairs, every new nurse you meet. It all drags you down just a little more. And when the optimism starts to fade, when new and worse issues keep popping up ... it gets to you. And when you finally recognize that look of grim acceptance in the doctors' faces, hear it in their voices ... the floor drops out from under you.

After the heart attack, she had been in a medicated coma for a while and they had a lot of trouble reviving her. When we got the call that she was awake and alert, I rushed right over with the kids.

She was smiling and laughing and all she wanted to do was play with her grandkids. Which was really nice for them, and nice for her, and frankly good for me to see. Don't ever pass up those opportunities, you never know when it'll be the last.

But, between you and me, I know the kids and the nurses couldn't tell, but she wasn't herself. She wasn't totally sure where she was or even who I was. But, man, she loved those kids. She smiled and laughed as they climbed on her. She listened intently as they told her all their silly kid stuff. She hung on every word. She was so happy.

She asked me to take a picture of her together with the kids. A photo? Really? Now? My instinct was to refuse. With her hair disheveled and her too pale skin, she barely resembled the woman who raised me.

In the end I did take the picture, and I'm really glad I did. It's a great shot. She's never looked happier, even with an oxygen tube on her face. And, now, it's the last picture I have of her.

A week later and the next trip to the ER, she couldn't speak. We gave her a pen and she wrote out a few things. She wanted to know where my wife and the grandkids were. She didn't ask about money or politics or religion or food or her health. She wanted to know where the kids were and that they were OK. She was in and out of consciousness and eventually was too exhausted to communicate.

Something told me that she might never come back. I was right.

A few days later, the doctors let us know they had run out of options. Her body was starting to shut down and any efforts at this point were more likely to hurt than help. We made the decision as a family to make her as comfortable as possible, and to wait.

Early that next morning I went back to the hospital to relieve my wife from sitting at my mom's bedside all night. As an aside, if you find a partner who will stay all night with your dying mother — marry that person. Do whatever you need to do to hang on to that person. My Wonderful Wife talked to my mom all night, sang to her, told her we loved her. She made sure the nurses were doing everything they could. She brushed my mom's hair and applied her favorite lip balm to keep her lips from drying and cracking. I am dumbfounded by the depth of the entire gesture. The Wonderful Wife says it was not a big deal, but I know it's a debt that can never truly be repaid.

So, after relieving my wife that morning I got to sit with my mom as she lay there, comatose, struggling to breathe, dying. I held her hand and I cried big, fat Viking tears. I told her we all loved her, and everything was good and she could leave. I told her that I was sorry for all of it, the millions of stupid things I had done, for every time I had gotten mad at her, for all the times I had disappointed her. I told her that none of it mattered anymore and I just wanted her to be at peace.

She never blinked or stirred. I had no indication to know if she could hear me. Was any part of my mother still in there? Was I being a fool by talking to this physical body that once had held my mother's essence? Was I an idiot for holding this limp hand that had once comforted me?

A couple hours later, my brother, his wife and my step-father came into the room, carrying sack lunches and ready to wait with her through to the end. I loudly announced for Mom that they had all arrived to see her. She took two more difficult, raspy breaths ... and was gone. They didn't even have time to set down their lunches.

It was so clear that she had waited. She knew. She had heard everything. Somewhere, deep inside there, she heard and she knew and she waited until we were all there before she let go.

So, yes, this morning I returned that envelope. I did exactly what my mom had taught me to do when I was little. Yes, I wanted to see what was inside it. Yes, it could have been a bunch of money or something sensational or wicked. But it wasn't mine to see. I didn't look inside and I gave it back to whom it belonged. It was a very minor inconvenience to my day but may have made a profound difference to the owner. Or, for all I know, it may have been just trash after all. Regardless, it made me feel normal, and good.

Back on that front porch, it turns out this is a small town and I had met the man and his wife at an event just a couple weeks before. We weren't friends on Facebook but they had seen the news about my mom on my wife's feed. They were gracious and kind and we chatted a little there on their stoop. Mostly we exchanged surprise that our lives had intersected in such an unexpected way.

Eventually, I wished them well and went home. It was a wonderful reminder that love and community are everywhere and will find you when you need them.

What else can you do when your mother dies? The woman who literally and figuratively made you, who fed and washed you, showed you how to dress yourself and tie your own shoes. How do you face a world that no longer includes the woman who taught you left from right, right from wrong? How do you leave the house when you've lost that one person who you knew would always be on your side, no matter how badly you screwed up?

Well, now I know what you do when your mother dies. I've always known, and you know it, too. You go on, doing all the things she taught you to do. You continue being the man she raised you to be.

She's not gone. Oh, no. She's here and alive in everything I do, every decision I make. I didn't realize it at the time, but it was her voice in my head that told me to pick up that envelope and drive it back to the owner. That voice also told me to not be too proud of myself for doing the right thing, that it should be expected and not rewarded. Her voice echoed in my head, telling me to not tell anyone what I had done because that would just be vanity and prideful on my part.

Well, except I am telling you about it. I don't always do what that little voice says. Having her guidance is good, but part of being my own person is realizing she wasn't always right. Seeking praise is not prideful, within reason. Asking for and accepting help is not shameful, but actually quite healthy. Admitting weakness is the greatest form of strength.

We all have the ability to question and refine our upbringings, to take the good and leave the bad, to improve and do better. I think one of my greatest goals in life is to improve on my parent's choices.

But, most importantly, I will continue to do what my mom cared about the most. And luckily for me, I'm already doing it. For years I had always anticipated, at the end of her life, that she would unleash that pent up guilt trip on me and that we would argue about religion. I dreaded it, but I was ready for that argument. But instead, she made it incredibly clear to me that her true wish is simply that I raise her grandchildren to be happy, productive and beautiful people. People who pick up and return envelopes.

And, just for the record, I'm teaching my son that some of the strongest, most masculine things he can do are to cry, to share his feelings and to ask for help. He's going to be a stronger man than me for it, and I'm very much OK with that. And so is that little voice in my head.

Go — live your life and be the person your mother wants you to be.

If she's alive, call her. If she's not, then remember her well. Tell your children and grandchildren stories about her and let her live on in her family's hearts.

She deserves it.

About The Author

Troy Maynard is a giant Viking, foodie, geeky gamer, father of three and master of none. Between frequent photographs of meals and occasional pillaging (alleged), he writes out his thoughts on life from his Mead Hall in the rolling hills of southern Indiana. Ransacking passing ships doesn't pay the bills, so he also works in the software industry, where he gets to use his tantrum management skills on a daily basis.

Find more stories and silliness on his blog, veryvocalviking.com, and his parenting column *My Dad Voice* in Limestone Post Magazine, limestonepostmagazine.com/author/troymaynard

Made in the USA
Columbia, SC
09 November 2017